BIBLE WOMEN SPEAK TO US TODAY

Mary E. Jensen

AUGSBURG Publishing House • Minneapolis

To my father,
the Reverend Lawrence W. Halvorson,
with love, gratitude, and joy

Contents

Preface

The women we meet in the pages of the Bible actually lived on this earth. They experienced the human drama in all its heights and depths, in all its joys and sorrows. Only when we know this will the activity of God in their lives have any meaning or significance for us. We recognize the truth of God's power and love when, for example, the joy of Elizabeth, the endurance of Leah, and the grief of Rizpah are seen as human, "just-like-me" experiences.

To demonstrate the "realness" of Bible women in these meditations, I have chosen to share some experiences from my own life. I hope they can be windows through which the Bible women may be seen in all their humanness. The blend of modern and ancient stories together with the application to our own lives becomes a doorway through which we are led to respond to the love, grace, and mercy of God in our Savior, Jesus Christ.

These meditations are not organized according to topic. Instead, as in life, joy, suffering, endurance, prayer, and praise occur together. The experiences of Bible women and the truths which can be learned from them are intermingled—the delightful and the reflective, the joyous and the sad, the earthly and the heavenly. Neither are the meditations organized according to the historical appearance of women in the Bible. The truths to be discovered in the women's lives are not dependent on their biblical order. Bible references are given to help the reader discover the entire passage and context in which the woman appears. Other activities are suggested to enrich the meditation and its application to our lives today.

These meditations, which explore God's eternal truths, may be read silently or aloud, in personal devotions or study, with family and friends, with small groups or large.

Like Mary Magdalene we can say, "I have seen the Lord!" And then, like Mary, we too can tell others about Jesus and his power and love (John 20:18).

Healed and Straightened in Christ
The Woman Who Was Bent Over

And there was a woman who had a spirit of infirmity for eighteen years; she was bent over and could not fully straighten herself. And when Jesus saw her, he called her and said to her, "Woman, you are freed from your infirmity." And he laid his hands upon her, and immediately she was made straight, and she praised God.   Luke 13:11-13

As a child I remember visiting my Aunt Thea. She was of great interest to me because, like the woman in Luke's gospel, Aunt Thea had to walk bent over. She was bent at the waist and could see only the ground. Aunt Thea probably was a tall woman, considering the rest of the family, but I only saw her bent over. My child heart felt deeply sorry for her, and I wondered how she could possibly do it, day after day.

Most of us are fortunate enough to be able to walk upright with only occasional muscle spasms or kinks in our backs. We can see the sky, people's faces, tops of trees, and tall buildings. But we are "bent over" in other ways. We are sinful people whose natural tendency is to look only downward and inward. It's natural for us to see only difficulties, problems, and bad news. It comes naturally to concentrate on the faults, the mistakes, and the shortcomings of other people, being judgmental of them. At the same time we as humans are prone to think selfishly, concentrating on what is good only for us and what pleases us, blissfully ignoring our own faults. Jesus addressed this situation when he spoke of the speck we notice in another person's eye while ignoring the log in our own (Matt. 7:4). We are naturally and inherently turned away from God and his light and truth. Even when we want to do better, we cannot (Rom. 7:19).

Theologians have a way of describing this "natural tendency to look down," this human state of being "bent over." The theological term is "original sin." We are all afflicted with it, and we cannot cure ourselves of it. Furthermore, we all sin more and more, unable to turn our lives around and do better. Like the woman in Luke's account, we are unable to straighten up.

The woman had not been able to stand straight for 18 years. Every day she walked bent over, seeing only the ground, her own feet, and the feet of other people. Perhaps the children made fun of her, imitating the way she walked. But she could do nothing else, so she had to continue walking bent over, enduring the pain, the teasing, and the constant view of the ground. There didn't seem to be hope of anything better.

One day Jesus came to the synagogue in the town where the woman lived. It was the Sabbath day and many people were at the synagogue to worship. When Jesus saw the woman, he had compassion on her. He declared that she was healed, he touched her, and "immediately she was made straight"! What a shock! What joy for the woman! Luke says that she praised God. Later in the passage he also says that the people around her rejoiced at all the glorious things that were done by Jesus.

Like the woman who could suddenly see the sky, the trees, and other people, we are given new life through Jesus' death and resurrection. God has done what human beings are incapable of doing. He has cleansed us of all unrighteousness and healed us of our sin. "There is therefore now no condemnation for those who are in Christ Jesus. For the law of the Spirit of life in Christ Jesus has set me free from the law of sin and death" (Rom. 8:1-2).

We are now free to look up. We are free to praise God. We are free to notice the joys, the needs, and the problems of other people. We are free to serve them. We are free to discover the beauty in this world, in ourselves, and in the human beings who make up our families, our communities, and our church.

"And he laid his hands upon her, and immediately she was made straight, and she praised God." We, too, are healed and straightened people. Let us praise God today, looking upward toward him and then turning to serve others.

Dear Lord Jesus, you have cleansed us and healed us of our brokenness, our sinfulness. Through your death and resurrection you have straightened us and freed us to look upward and praise you all our days. Lord, give us eyes to notice the needs of other people. Give us ears to hear their words. Give us lips to bring your message of joy and comfort. Give us arms to share your healing and love. This day, Lord, renew us and refresh us with your grace and your peace.

To learn more about the healing of the woman who was bent over, as well as our own healing:
- Read Luke 13:10-17.
- Read Romans 8.
- Walk bent over for two or three minutes. What do you see? What can't you see? How would it feel if you knew you could never straighten up?
- Praise God for your health and walk straight and tall for the rest of the day.
- Praise God for your salvation in Jesus Christ and tell someone about it today.

Trust in the Lord's Timetable
Elizabeth

After these days his wife Elizabeth conceived, and for five months she hid herself, saying, "Thus the Lord has done to me in the days when he looked on me, to take away my reproach among men." . . . And when Elizabeth heard the greeting of Mary, the babe leaped in her womb; and Elizabeth was filled with the Holy Spirit and she exclaimed with a loud cry, "Blessed are you among women, and blessed is the fruit of your womb!"

Luke 1:24-25, 41-42

When my husband graduated from college, he applied at several universities for graduate fellowships and assistantships in mathematics. He also applied at the theological seminary, mostly because his college roommate did. The summer following graduation was a discouraging time. While Andy worked in a sausage factory in Maine, one door after another closed at the universities.

By the end of the summer he headed for Dubuque, Iowa, because the seminary was the only school which had accepted his application. The first two years of theological study were difficult; Andy came very close to dropping out.

His internship took us to Superior, Wisconsin, where Pastor Norm Engebretson was his supervisor. Norm sensed the struggle Andy was having. He assigned the young seminarian to two hours of daily Bible study and gave him all sorts of opportunities to meet and serve the people in the parish. By the time a year had passed under the influence of God's Word, the people of the church, and a compassionate pastor, Andy couldn't wait to get into the ministry full time.

In all his parishes, my husband has sensed the leading of the Holy Spirit in regard to education, experience, people, tasks, and ministry. Andy's future and profession had been a great puzzle with the pieces all jumbled up. It gradually became clear that we were waiting on the Lord's time, the Lord's plan, and, through it all, the Lord's strength.

Elizabeth was discouraged and unhappy. In all her years of marriage to Zechariah she had not been able to conceive a child. In Elizabeth's time and culture this was disastrous. A woman's identity and security were tied up in her children, particularly the boys. A woman was much to be pitied if she was childless. So Elizabeth not only had to deal with her personal sorrow, but she had to bear the pity and even the ridicule and scorn of other people.

Then one day Zechariah heard the marvelous word of the Lord: he and Elizabeth would be the parents of a son! Zechariah couldn't believe it. As a sign the Lord took away his speech until the child arrived. Elizabeth must have been just as incredulous. After all these years, she would *now* have a *baby?*

The miracle occurred, and Elizabeth was indeed pregnant. She must have alternated between great joy and great concern. Obviously the Lord had acted, but what did it all mean? How would she cope? Would she be healthy and strong enough to bear and raise a child?

One day Elizabeth received an affirmation of the Lord's purpose and plan. Her cousin Mary came to visit, and Elizabeth's baby leaped in her womb. She was filled with the Holy Spirit, and suddenly she knew of the child Mary was carrying and of the Lord's plan in *her* life. Elizabeth's baby, John, was to be the one who prepared the way for Jesus. The Lord's plan, the Lord's timetable, was perfect.

Life is so often a painful mystery. Bitter disappointments, broken dreams, and shattered plans litter our lives. When things don't happen according to our timetable, we can become impatient and angry. Even when we confess our faith in the Lord, it's often difficult to accept his way of accomplishing things and his timing.

We are not robots who go in whatever direction the Master

Programmer may send us. God has given us the ability to think and plan, as well as the gift of free will. He wants us to use our abilities and gifts. But God also wants us to know that his will for our lives is perfect and gracious. He asks us to give our lives to him so his perfect plan can be worked out through us. Yes, we can rebel and refuse to have any part in God's plan. But our true joy, our real fulfillment as God's children comes when we daily submit our will, our plans, and our lives to the Lord. Then it is possible to relax peacefully in the knowledge that the Lord in his perfect wisdom will always care for us and bless us.

Besides that, the adventure of living in the Lord is tremendous! You never know what growing and exciting experience is right around the corner. Of course there are sorrows and problems. We still live in the sinful world. But when our lives are hidden in the Lord, he can use even the worst tragedies for his glory. That is our hope and our trust. That is what brings us joy in the morning as we glorify God for another day to serve and love him.

Dear loving Lord, we try so hard to plan our lives, to be self-sufficient. Help us give our lives totally to you, and give us peace and joy in knowing that we are part of your perfect plan. Use our lives to your glory, Lord. Thank you for the joyous adventure of life lived in and for you.

To learn more about Elizabeth and John, as well as about trust in the Lord:
- Read Luke 1:5-80; Matt. 3:1-17; John 1:19-37; 3:22-30; Matt. 4:12-17; 11:2-19; 14:1-12.
- Read Psalm 27. Note all the wonderful nouns and verbs which describe God's loving actions. Memorize verses 1 and 14. Ask the Lord for peace and for trust. Ask not just once, but every time you sense the worries are coming back.

Endurance Produces Character
Leah

So Jacob went in to Rachel also, and he loved Rachel more than Leah, and served Laban for another seven years. When the Lord saw that Leah was hated, he opened her womb; but Rachel was barren.   Gen. 29:30-31

My son Joel doesn't care much for lemonade, and I think I know why. Of the three boys, he's the one who has heard my favorite saying the most often: "When you're handed a lemon—make lemonade!" It's really easy to give that kind of advice when you yourself are not facing an immovable object or an unchangeable situation.

Immovable objects make me think of the wall behind the parsonage. In 1980 we moved from a house on a large piece of land in Minnesota to a house on a narrow strip of land in Los Angeles. When I looked out my kitchen window in Minnesota, I saw a lovely green lawn, a pine tree, Russian olive trees, and, at various times of year, tulips, peonies, geraniums, or wide expanses of snow. Out my kitchen window in Los Angeles I could see a weathered cement-block wall about 12 feet from the house. There is no grass here; cement is laid from the house to the wall. It's a handy patio, but, accustomed to a spacious backyard, I found it devastating. For a year I stared with sorrow at the ugly gray wall. It was so—permanent! It became a symbol of everything I had left in Minnesota. Finally it occurred to me that I would have to make lemonade. That's what I always told everyone else!

First I painted the whole wall "wicker tan." Then I sketched on paper a prototype of what I would draw on my wall: flowers, a rainbow, vines, elves, butterflies, birds, a ladybug, a palm tree—even a pot of gold at the end of the rainbow. I have spent many hours painting the wall behind the parsonage, and now I look out on a glorious scene. It's even inspired me to plant orange trees in tubs, set out bright geraniums in pots, and hang a bougainvillea plant—right outside my kitchen window. I couldn't change the wall, but I could do things to help my attitude about it.

Leah was the older of Laban's two girls. It seemed only right to Laban that Leah be married first, so he tricked Jacob into marrying her. Eventually Jacob was married to both sisters, but all through her life Leah had to live with the fact that Jacob and Rachel had a special love for each other. The Lord gave Leah many children to make up for the fact that she was hated, but somehow Leah had to deal daily with her misery. It had to be very painful to know her husband didn't love her, that her sister was the favorite, to hear them be happy together. Leah remained with Jacob, but she didn't really have any other choice—as a woman in that culture she was forced to deal with a difficult situation.

Rachel died in childbirth, and at last Leah became Jacob's only wife. When he was about to die, Jacob requested to be buried with Leah, in the same place as Abraham and Isaac. Perhaps the years following Rachel's death were easier ones for Leah. In any case, the priesthood of Israel sprang from Leah's son Levi, and her son Judah was the ancestor of Boaz, David, and the Messiah.

Having lived on this earth a shade more than four decades, I'm beginning to understand what Paul meant when he said that suffering produces endurance, endurance produces character, and character produces hope (Rom. 5:3-4). The very things that are difficult for us, which we would love to escape, are the things which make us strong. There are things in life which cannot be changed: one's physical appearance; certain physical, mental, or emotional handicaps; one's talents or lack of them; illnesses and deaths of loved ones and of oneself. Certain relationships cannot be changed, and neither can certain circumstances of one's life. Christians have to realize that they live on a sinful earth and are affected by the results of sin, evil, and death. We claim the victory of Christ over these things for all eternity, but we still must deal with the reality of them for a time on this earth.

How do we do that? We bring our immovable objects and unchangeable situations to the Lord in prayer, asking him to purify us through our endurance and to remove bitterness and anger. We ask the Lord to show us what can be done in the situation and to calm our hearts in regard to that which cannot be changed. This healing and renewal of our attitudes must occur daily. The Lord gives us joy and peace in daily doses. Gradually we will discover that as a result of the difficulty and of God's grace infused through it we have grown in character and strength. Then we know that God does indeed love us and will continue to work in our lives. My beautiful wall reminds me each day of God's love and mercy in a "set-in-concrete" situation.

Dear Lord Jesus, sometimes life seems so unfair. People are afflicted with problems and situations which cannot be controlled. Lord, if it be your will, remove obstacles and problems from our lives, but regardless, grant us peace in the midst of difficulties, removing anger and bitterness. Thank you, Jesus, for giving your life to save us from the eternal ravages of sin and evil. Be with us as we suffer a little while on this earth.

To learn more about Leah and also about suffering:
- Read Genesis 29–32; 49:28-33.
- Read 1 Peter 1:3-9; 2:18-25; 3:13-22; 4:1-19; 5:1-11.
- Think carefully about the possibilities of positive, upbuilding action which might be taken in your particular "unchangeable situation." Ask the Lord to show you the way. In the meantime, ask the Lord for a new attitude. Read Psalm 51.

Teaching through a Christ-filled Life
Dorcas

So Peter rose and went with them. And when he had come, they took him to the upper room. All the widows stood beside him weeping, and showing coats and garments which Dorcas made while she was with them. But Peter put them all outside and knelt down and prayed; then turning to the body he said, "Tabitha, rise." And she opened her eyes, and when she saw Peter she sat up. And he gave her his hand and lifted her up. Then calling the saints and widows he presented her alive. And it became known throughout all Joppa, and many believed in the Lord.   Acts 9:39-42

I have a friend whose life radiates her faith in Jesus Christ. She doesn't even realize what a clear witness she gives of the Lord in everything she says and does. She often speaks of her Savior in warm and vital terms, but he glows through her attitudes and actions even more than through her words.

My friend is relaxed about herself. Her poise and confidence come not from a "finishing school" or a self-improvement course but from her sure knowledge that Jesus loves her and has freed her from her sins. Such freedom and confidence allow her to forget herself and concentrate on other people. And this she does with joy and patience. No one will ever know how many encouraging notes she has written to discouraged, sorrowing, hurting, or disappointed people. No one could count the phone calls and friendly visits she has made, or the large and small favors she has done for others. She is loved, admired, respected, and enjoyed by young and old alike. My friend is like a beautiful stained-glass window through which God's Son shines with great clarity.

Once in a while we are privileged to be blessed by such people.

They become shining beacons to us in what is often a gloomy world. They embody Christ's love and light in a special way.

Dorcas was a person like that. The people in Joppa loved her. Dorcas used her special talent for sewing to make coats and garments for the people, especially the widows and their families. But Dorcas became ill and died. The sorrowing women gently cared for her body and laid it in an upper room while an urgent message was sent to Peter to come to Joppa. When he arrived, he prayed for Dorcas and then commanded her body to arise. And the incredible miracle happened! Dorcas was brought back to life by the Lord. Imagine the surprise and the joy of the widows! Imagine first the disbelief and then the amazed understanding of the townspeople. Dorcas who had been dead was alive again.

Dorcas had a second life. What joy this "new life" was to the Christians in Joppa! And what a powerful witness it was to the unbelievers. Many people believed in the Lord Jesus because of the living, breathing miracle walking among them. Acts does not attribute a single word to Dorcas but tells about her beautiful first life and her faith-inspiring second life from the viewpoint of others.

James encourages us to demonstrate God's wisdom in our lives: "Who is wise and understanding among you? By his good life let him show his works in the meekness of wisdom. . . . But the wisdom from above is first pure, then peaceable, gentle, open to reason, full of mercy and good fruits, without uncertainty or insincerity" (James 3:13, 17).

If we are trying on our own to be good people, to be happy, wise, and perfect in all we do and say, we will fail miserably. It isn't possible for human beings to lead model lives, to "keep the law perfectly." But if Christ is the center, the controlling master of our thoughts, beliefs, and attitudes—our lives will naturally show forth the fruits of God's Spirit. James has mentioned some of these fruits—purity, peace, gentleness, willingness to listen, mercy. The Apostle Paul tells about others—love, joy, patience, kindness, faithfulness, self-control (Gal. 5:22-23).

The Christ-filled life teaches other people about our Lord and

Savior. And not only is it a *teaching* tool—it is a *doing* tool. Believers are Christ's body here on earth. We are his hands and feet, his touch and smile, his voice and his warmth. Keeping close to the Lord through worship, Word, sacrament, and prayer, we will find that he fills us with his life-giving, life-*living* power and grace.

Dear Lord Jesus, fill our lives with the gifts of your Holy Spirit. We do not naturally live in purity and peace, in love and mercy. It is only through your gifts that we can show forth the beauty of your grace and truth. May our Christ-filled lives be beautiful instruments of witness and care to all we meet. Lord, increase your love and mercy in our lives; decrease our pride and fear.

To learn more about Dorcas, as well as about the Christ-filled life:

- Read Acts 9:32-43. Now read Acts 10 to note the next step in Peter's ministry. The raising of Dorcas had a powerful effect on Peter, too!
- Do some scripture research on the fruits of the Spirit. Read Gal. 5:16, 22-23. Then, using a concordance, meditate on passages about patience, kindness, joy, etc. Ask the Lord to bring forth these fruits in your life.

Today's Opportunities
Queen Esther

Then Mordecai told them to return answer to Esther, "Think not that in the king's palace you will escape any more than all the other Jews. For if you keep silence at such a time as this, relief and deliverance will rise for the Jews from another quarter, but you and your father's house will perish. And who knows whether you have not come to the kingdom for such a time as this?"   Esther 4:13-14

"What is a nice girl like you doing in a place like this?" The television advertisement for an oven cleaner shows a doleful housewife framed in a crusty, dirty oven. Sometimes we wonder what *we* are doing in difficult situations or circumstances. These circumstances may be of our own making or they may have simply happened to us, but once in them we often see no way out. We feel trapped and used by other people. There seems to be no hope or future in the situation. We long for a miracle that will easily and instantly free us from the difficult and unwanted circumstance.

Perhaps the circumstance involves perplexing family or marital problems. Perhaps it's an illness or handicap which afflicts us or a family member. Perhaps it's a working condition, neighborhood situation, or church problem that seems intolerable.

"What is a nice girl like you doing in a place like this?" The young Jewish queen in ancient Persia probably wondered what *she* was doing in the king's palace when all the trouble broke out. The evil Haman had influenced the king to annihilate all the Jews in the country. Queen Esther's cousin, Mordecai, who had raised her as his adopted daughter, begged her to intercede with the king for her people. At first Esther was hesitant to try, but Mordecai reminded her of God's power. Then he declared that God may actually have placed Esther in the palace as queen just

21

for the purpose of helping her people in their desperate hour of need.

With the encouragement and strong words of her cousin, Esther approached the problem bravely. She began to treat it as an opportunity and as a challenge. Esther looked about and carefully planned her actions. She prayed to the Lord of Israel and implored others to pray for her as she carried out her plan. Queen Esther used her difficult position and circumstance as a positive opportunity for good.

What about our own situations? Are we spending too much time lamenting over the problems and moaning about how difficult everything seems to be? Are we feeling sorry for ourselves, concentrating all our attention inward? It's time to remember Mordecai's words to Esther as she trembled indecisively in the palace: "And who knows whether you have not come to the kingdom for such a time as this?"

Think about it: perhaps you possess just the talent, just the attitude, just the opportunity, just the position, just the relationship, just the strength, just the motivation it will take to solve this problem or to be an instrument of the Lord to use it for good. Perhaps God has led you to this place in your life for a purpose. Ask the Lord to show you how you can be his servant in this situation and then ask for the gifts of grace you will need to carry out his will.

Perhaps you will need more patience or more energy. Perhaps you need to talk less and listen more. Perhaps you need to reach out to someone in a positive way, leaving your own defenses behind. Perhaps it's simply a matter of smiling, or touching, or just being there.

What *opportunities* are facing you today? In what way will you be the hands, the feet, the voice, and the touch of the Lord in your situation in life? How can God use you in this time, in this place?

Dear Lord Jesus, nothing is perfect in our world, but you have promised to be with us every step of the way. Today give us your grace and your strength to face our particular situations and our special problems. May your love shine through us, helping us to lift the burdens in this world for your name's sake.

To learn more about Queen Esther and about acting positively in our situations:

- Read all 10 chapters of the Book of Esther.
- Ask a Jewish friend about the festival of Purim.
- Read Phil. 4:4-9; Gal. 5:22-26; 1 Peter 1:13—2:3.

Specific Prayers
Hannah

And [Hannah] vowed a vow and said, "O Lord of hosts, if thou wilt indeed look on the affliction of thy maidservant, and remember me, and not forget thy maidservant, but wilt give to thy maidservant a son, then I will give him to the Lord all the days of his life, and no razor shall touch his head." . . . And in due time Hannah conceived and bore a son, and she called his name Samuel, for she said, "I have asked him of the Lord."
1 Sam. 1:11, 20

Rummaging through old files, I came across a booklet entitled "38 Years with a Prayer List." Memories flooded back as I examined it. My mother had given it to me when I was 16 years old and knew everything. "This is something I've found to be very helpful," she said. "Maybe you'd like it, too." I remember glancing at it and then putting it away. A prayer list? How dull. Now, however, I read each word about the anonymous author's experiences in recording his petitions and noting when and how the prayers were answered. He told some amazing stories. I decided to try it myself.

Now I have a prayer list which is very full and very marked up. It is loaded with various petitions to the Lord. Some are quite ordinary: "Lord, keep me safe as I drive to San Bernardino tomorrow." Other petitions are momentous: "Lord Jesus, please help our church find just the right business and school administrators." Many petitions are for others: "Lord, give Dan comfort as he mourns Norma's death." "Heavenly Father, please be with Dick and Karol and baby Deborah in a special way." Other petitions are very personal: "Lord God, sometimes I say such sharp words. Please give me patience and loving, caring words."

Writing the prayers down forces me to formulate my ideas and speak to the Lord about them. Each petition is dated. When the prayer is answered, I note the date and the result and then draw lines through the petition. I never cross it out, because I've found great joy and increased confidence in the Lord when I go back and see—literally *see*—all the answered prayers. Furthermore, I've discovered that my prayer list is a "burial ground" for my worries. *There, I wrote it down. I've brought it to the Lord. He will take care of the situation.*

Hannah was desperate and miserable. She was childless even after many years of marriage to Elkanah. To make matters worse, her rival, Peninnah, Elkanah's other wife, had many children and tormented Hannah about her childlessness. One day Hannah brought a special petition to the God of Israel. She pleaded with the Lord to see her plight and give her a son, and then she vowed to give the child back to the Lord.

Once she had brought her petition to the Lord, Hannah felt a great sense of relief. "Then the woman went her way and ate, and her countenance was no longer sad" (1 Sam. 1:18). Eventually Hannah "conceived and bore a son, and she called his name Samuel, for she said, 'I have asked him of the Lord.'"

One thing I've come to understand about prayer is that God is like a loving parent who wants me in his presence. Yes, he knows what I need and want even before I ask, but, like a parent, he wants me to verbalize it and communicate with him. Not only does this bring joy to the Lord—it brings great joy and peace to me. Prayer is a gift of God for my well-being.

Also, I've learned that when God doesn't answer my prayers exactly to my liking it's not because he doesn't hear or because he doesn't care. It's because he loves me so much that he won't grant something harmful or wrong for me just because I've asked for it. Again, we see the quality of a loving parent who wants to hear every concern, every problem, every worry. The parent will listen but will do only what is best for the child.

And finally, I've come to realize that God responds to my prayers in many ways. By writing down my petitions I can actually *see* what God is doing in my life. I've noticed that his answer often comes through the touch or the voice or the action of another person. Far from being unresponsive, the Lord is constantly active all about me.

Hannah brought her special petition to the Lord with humbleness and faith. We, too, can be specific and trusting in our prayers. We can share all the worries, all the fun, all the delight, all the concerns. Nothing is too great or too small for our God. "Have no anxiety about anything, but in everything by prayer and supplication with thanksgiving let your requests be made known to God" (Phil. 4:6).

Dear Lord Jesus, so often we are spiritually deaf and blind. Open our eyes, open our ears to your loving activity in our lives. Today we claim the promise that you will always hear us when we pray. Please show us your love and mercy as we bring our petitions to you. Thank you for hearing us, Lord. Strengthen our faith and give us grace for this day.

To learn more about Hannah and also more about prayer:
- Read 1 Samuel 1–3.
- Read Matt. 7:7-11; 6:5-15; James 4:2; 5:16.
- Try using a prayer list. Write down brief petitions, dating them. Then date the prayers when they are answered, lightly drawing a line through them. Save all your prayer lists. Reread them often for joy and confidence in the Lord.

Trust and Obedience Are the Keys
The Widow at Zarephath

*And [the widow] went and did as Elijah said; and she, and he,
and her household ate for many days. The jar of meal was not
spent, neither did the cruse of oil fail, according to the word of
the Lord which he spoke by Elijah.   1 Kings 17:15-16*

When our oldest son Dan was five years old, he was diagnosed
as having multiple allergies resulting in asthma. According to
the skin tests, the child was allergic to every inhalant (things
breathed into the system) except silk and human hair. The doctor
warned us that treatment for allergies, especially severe ones like
Dan's, is not always effective and that desensitization shots might
or might not be the answer for our son's condition. But the doctor
recommended that the shots be tried anyway, and we as worried
parents were quick to obey.

For about two years the desensitization shots were given weekly
in ever-increasing dosages. After that Dan was on maintenance
dosage for another three years. At first we did not see any improve-
ment at all. In fact, it was more than a year before we started
noticing that his color was better and he wasn't having the difficult
asthmatic breathing with his colds. Gradually Dan began growing and gaining weight; in two years his whole disposition
changed; by the end of the five years Dan was the specialist's
prime example of the effectiveness of desensitization treatment.
Today Dan is 21 years old, stands nearly six feet, seven inches
tall, and plays basketball for Dana College in Blair, Nebraska.

Our health, our happiness, and our well-being are not usually
provided in huge, one-time dosages. We find our needs are or-
dinarily met day by day—sometimes, in crises, even minute by
minute. It is no simple play on words when we ask God to "give
us *this day* our *daily* bread."

There was a woman in ancient Israel who experienced the marvel of being fed by the Lord day by day. A terrible drought and famine occurred as a judgment upon King Ahab and the people for their idol worship. A widow in the town of Zarephath had only a handful of meal and a little oil left, and because they had no way of getting more food, she and her son were prepared to die.

But God intervened in a miraculous way. The prophet Elijah asked the widow for water and food. She told him she had very little—in fact, she was preparing to make the meal and oil into a little cake for the last piece of food she and her son would eat. But Elijah persisted: "Fear not; go and do as you have said; but first make me a little cake of it and bring it to me, and afterward make for yourself and your son" (1 Kings 17:13). The widow obeyed and to her amazement discovered that she still had meal and oil left. In fact, every day there was meal and oil available in the containers which had seemed destined to be quickly emptied. And not only did the widow and her son eat, but also Elijah and the other people in her household.

This story reminds us of the manna the Israelites received every day in the wilderness. They were instructed to gather only enough for a day's food for their household; any extra would rot.

The Lord wants us to trust him, to rely totally on him. God teaches this by allowing us to discover that we cannot provide for ourselves and by showing us that he himself provides what we need *as we need it*. We learn to depend on the Lord, trusting his promises because we've experienced his faithfulness. We are thus led to greater heights of trust.

This trust involves obedience. For us as parents, it meant following the doctor's orders of weekly injections, even when we saw no results. For the widow of Zarephath, it meant giving her last portion of meal and oil to Elijah. For the believer, it means putting aside, by God's grace, the sinful "I can do it myself, I don't need any help" attitude and resting in the Lord's love and care each day. This is true in all areas of our lives: physical needs, health, relationships, emotions, problems, work, and hobbies.

Jesus taught us not to be anxious but to let each day care for itself (Matt. 6:34). Peter counseled us to "Cast all your anxieties on him, for he cares about you" (1 Peter 5:7).

Remember that everything will not be solved at once. We receive grace and strength *for that moment, for that day*. Gradually, looking back, we realize how faithfully the Lord has kept us and know for a certainty that God will provide for the next day's needs in his own way, in his own time.

Live each day to the fullest. Trust God for all you need, obeying his request to humble yourself under his yoke. You'll discover it's a yoke of joy and peace which is smoothed to perfect comfort by God's daily provisions of love and mercy.

Dear Lord Jesus, you have asked us to come to you, knowing we labor and are heavy laden. You have promised us rest even as we wear your beautiful yoke. Today, Lord, give us peace in the knowledge that you love us and will have mercy on us. Take away all thoughts of self-sufficiency which deny our need of you, and forgive us for not trusting your promises. Thank you for the rest, the joy, the freedom you provide.

To learn more about the widow of Zarephath, as well as about trust and obedience:
- Read 1 Kings 17. Be sure to notice that the widow obeyed before she trusted or believed.
- Read Psalm 62; Matt. 6:25-34; 1 Peter 1:1-2; Acts 5:12-42.
- Learn the hymn "Trust and Obey." (Look in a youth or gospel songbook.)

Love Gives a Warning
Pilate's Wife

So when they gathered, Pilate said to them, "Whom do you want me to release for you, Barabbas or Jesus who is called Christ?" For he knew that it was out of envy that they had delivered him up. Besides, while he was sitting on the judgment seat, his wife sent word to him, "Have nothing to do with that righteous man, for I have suffered much over him today in a dream." Matt. 27:17-19

In Minnesota in the spring we would hear discussions on the radio about the importance of the tornado watch and the tornado warning. A watch simply meant that weather conditions were ripe for the formation of funnel clouds and tornadoes. A warning meant that a tornado had actually been sighted somewhere, and then a loud blaring horn would sound on the radio. Most communities in Minnesota were equipped with similar blaring horns to warn residents of the impending danger. I knew tornadoes were dangerous; I'd seen tornado damage. Yet whenever I heard the blaring horn, my first reaction was to run to the door or window to see if I could spot the funnel cloud. I can remember only once when I actually went to the basement, the recommended procedure.

One afternoon in June 1980 a tornado warning was sounded. We stood on the front lawn watching the sky get pitch black over the neighboring town. Sure enough, a tornado ripped through parts of Bloomington that day, even while we watched from our yard in Burnsville. Yes, we knew the danger and the recommended action, but still we stood in our yard and watched. The warning had been given, but we ignored it.

Pontius Pilate was also given a warning. The prisoner Jesus had been delivered to him by the chief priests and elders of the

Jews. From questioning him, Pilate knew that Jesus did not deserve to die, but the religious leaders were insistent. They were even beginning to hint that if he didn't cooperate they might go over Pilate's head to Rome.

In the midst of his deliberations, Pilate's wife sent him a warning. By means of a strange and nightmarish dream she had become convinced that her husband must have nothing to do with Jesus; she knew that Pilate would regret it deeply if he did.

The governor tried to get out of the situation. He offered the people a choice between Jesus and a known criminal, Barabbas, thinking the people would choose Jesus to be released. But the religious leaders persuaded the people to ask for Barabbas. Now the governor was in dire straits: if he released Jesus, he must face the anger of the Jewish leaders and also repercussions from Rome; if he sentenced Jesus to die, he would know that justice had not been served. Pilate did what he believed to be the next best thing: he literally washed his hands of the situation, and Jesus was led off to be crucified by the people.

Pilate's wife gave a warning, but it was not heeded. According to tradition, Pilate did indeed live to regret the day he met Jesus. He was eventually stripped of his office and banished.

We are all good at brushing off warnings and advice. Children ignore parents and teachers. Adults ignore warnings from government officials, doctors, lawyers, and pastors. We believe that we are in control, that we can manage our own lives. This happens with God's warnings in the Scripture, too. We enjoy hearing about God's love and mercy, but warnings about sin and sinful behavior are not quite so pleasing to us. We tend to think they're for other people. We also tend to think that laws in the Scripture do not really apply to Christians. After all, didn't Christ free us from all that?

The laws of nature and the course of human events guarantee that certain results will come from certain actions. Every mother has told her child, "You must stay out of the street or a car will hit you!" Or she has said, "Don't touch that hot stove! You'll get burned!" Paul lists the works of the flesh in Galatians 5, including fornication, strife, envy, and drunkenness. God warns against gratifying the desires of the flesh, because he knows we will hurt ourselves. The natural results of fornication are venereal disease, unwanted pregnancy, broken relationships, shame, guilt, physical pain, or even death. Drunkenness can result in damaged internal organs, destruction of brain cells, and behavior which hurts or even kills other people. Humans tend to believe that God is being mean and unfair when he warns, even commands, against certain behavior and attitudes.

God warns us against sinful behavior because he loves us. The warnings and laws are for our benefit and well-being. It's easy to skip over God's warnings, going on to passages about love. What we need to learn anew is that God's warnings *are* messages of love, designed to help us live joyful, productive, righteous lives on this earth and for all eternity.

Dear Lord God, we know you love and care for us. Your love is in your laws and commands as well as in your Son, Jesus, who came to perfectly fulfill the law. Lord, give us strength to heed your warnings and to lead lives pleasing to you.

To learn more about Pilate, his wife, and God's loving warnings:
- Read Matt. 27:1-2, 11-26; Mark 15:1-15; Luke 23:1-25; John 18:28—19:16.
- Read Rom. 6:15-23; 8:1-17; 12:1-2.
- Examine your attitudes and reactions toward warnings, whether from God or humans. What do you learn about yourself? What action or change is indicated? Ask God to help you do it. And thank him for his great love.

Inspiration and Perspiration
Jochebed

And when [Jochebed] could hide him no longer she took for him a basket made of bulrushes, and daubed it with bitumen and pitch; and she put the child in it and placed it among the reeds at the river's brink. And his sister stood at a distance, to know what would be done to him.   Exod. 2:3-4

A popular phrase from my high school Bible camping days has stuck with me over the years. "Pray as if everything depended upon God; then work as if everything depended upon you." I remember being impressed with the idea that I had a great responsibility in my life situations, but that prayer always needed to precede my efforts. I also remember becoming aware that my thinking, common sense, physical abilities, and talents were all God-given and that God expected me to use them to the fullest. Up until then I had thought that somehow God would work his will without my involvement.

Jochebed knew it was a miracle that her little son was even alive, because the king of Egypt had ordered all male Hebrew babies to be killed. Somehow she had hidden the baby, but the infant was growing and she feared that his cries would attract attention. How could she save the little boy? The desperate mother undoubtedly asked the God of Israel to help her, but Jochebed did not wait for angels to spirit the baby away or for a great lightning bolt to strike the pharaoh. She took matters into her own hands.

Knowing that the pharaoh's daughter bathed in the river, Jochebed decided to bring the baby to her attention, hoping the princess would save him. Jochebed found a little basket of papyrus reeds and made it watertight with the sticky bitumen and pitch. Little baskets like these apparently were quite common in Egypt and served to hold images of gods. Perhaps Jochebed intentionally used an Egyptian-type basket which would not attract undue attention but at the same time would be interesting to the princess. And then she placed the baby in the basket and floated the basket in the marshy part of the river. The baby's sister was given the task of watching the precious basket.

Pharaoh's daughter came to bathe, and the basket did indeed catch her eye. When the princess saw the little boy in the basket, she knew it must be one of the Hebrew babies. Jochebed's prayers were answered in a wonderful way. Not only was her little son saved, but she was able to nurse him and care for him until he was old enough to live in the palace. Pharaoh's daughter adopted the child as her own, and Moses grew up in the king's household.

What a miracle! God preserved and protected the life of the baby who would grow up to be a great leader in Israel. And the miracle came about through prayer and through the determination and ingenuity of Moses' mother, Jochebed. She prayed, asking God to save her baby. But the matter didn't rest there: Jochebed put her baby in a basket and attracted the attention of a princess.

Possessing a vital Christian faith does not eliminate our responsibilities. God has blessed us with talents, gifts, and opportunities to use in his service. We ask the Lord through his Holy Spirit to give us the strength and the wisdom to use these gifts well—and then we get to work!

The Apostle Paul used the beautiful image of the body of Christ to describe the relationship of believers to Christ and to each other. This is not simply an interesting picture; it has important implications for "inspiration and perspiration" in our Christian lives. It is the human body which is able to walk, talk, think, carry, hug, and smile. Believers in Christ are asked to be active on this earth, serving Christ. We are God's hands and feet, arms and legs, voice and smile to the people we meet. We are the body of Christ. It is not enough only to bask in the comfort of Bible study and prayer; we are also called to use our gifts and opportunities to their fullest in our particular situations and circumstances.

Morning prayer time gives direction and *inspiration* for the day. And the day is to be filled with the *"perspiration"* of serving the Lord in all we do. The gifts of reasoning, common sense, imagination, and physical capabilities all enable us to carry out the Lord's will.

What is a problem or concern for you today? First ask the Lord's Holy Spirit to work his will in the situation, and ask for the wisdom and the capability to handle the problem in the best possible way. Then roll up your sleeves and take a deep breath. There's work to be done in Jesus' name and in the power of the Spirit!

Dear Lord God, you have blessed us in so many wonderful ways. Thank you for your Word and for the gift of prayer by which you communicate with us. Thank you for the intellectual and physical gifts you have given. Dear Lord, now we ask for wisdom to use these gifts wisely in our particular circumstances. Give us your grace to do your will today.

To learn more about Moses' family, the body of Christ, and the Holy Spirit:
- Read Exodus 2:1-10; 6:16-20, 26-27; 15:1-21; Numbers 12.
- Read 1 Corinthians 12.
- Read John 14:15-18, 25-27; 16:4-15. Note all the action words. The Holy Spirit truly works in us to give us comfort, guidance, and power.

Loving and Serving Result in Healing
Ruth

But Boaz answered [Ruth], "All that you have done for your mother-in-law since the death of your husband has been fully told me, and how you left your father and mother and your native land and came to a people that you did not know before. The Lord recompense you for what you have done, and a full reward be given you by the Lord, the God of Israel, under whose wings you have come to take refuge!"   Ruth 2:11-12

Marj was in a far country when Norm died. They had been serving a congregation in Okinawa for nearly three years. While on active duty in the Navy chaplaincy in Tokyo, Norm died of a massive heart attack, and Marj had to cope with a situation which left her without a husband and without a home. One teenage son was with her; the other was already in college in the United States. Marj and Peter came to Minneapolis to be near the college son. But the days were dark and difficult. What meaning could her life—once so full of husband, family, and church service—possibly have now?

Norm had been my husband's intern pastor, and we shared with Marj our grief and our memories of Norm. "What now?" was her question. "What purpose and meaning can my life have now?" At first all we could do was love her and assure her of God's love in her sorrow. Marj moved to the Minneapolis suburb where we lived and were serving a congregation. And little by little we saw it happen. First Marj began to help my husband with the confirmation program. It involved only some typing and telephoning, but it was a start. Then she began helping in the confirmation resource center, having contact with the young people. Soon she was working with the church school youngsters and their parents. Before long Marj was helping the church school teachers. Then we heard she was having lunch with other new widows, sharing her experience and her new life. The volunteer work led to a salaried position in which Marj could devote full time to organizing the education program in the large congregation. People came to love her, depending on her expertise and her wise counsel and strength. Marj's laugh and sense of humor became nearly as well known as her skill in education. Things could never ever be the same for Marj after Norm's death, and there was no way he could be replaced in her life. But Marj found a new area of service, a new way of living, and she found it through giving her life to other people.

When we suffer loss of any kind, our natural response is to look inward, to dwell on the pain and on the difficult situation. But healing and joy come only when our attention is directed toward other people, toward loving and serving them.

Ruth's husband died in Moab after about 10 years of marriage. Because she had lost her husband and both her sons, Naomi, Ruth's mother-in-law, wanted to return to her home in Bethlehem. Although a Moabitess and a stranger in Israel, Ruth insisted on going to Bethlehem with Naomi.

After the long journey, Ruth needed to support her mother-in-law and herself, so she picked up the leftover grain in the fields of Boaz. Day by day Ruth worked to find food and then help Naomi as they struggled to survive as two widows. Eventually Ruth married Boaz, who recognized her unselfish and giving spirit. Obed was born to Ruth and Boaz; Obed was the grandfather of King David. Even though she was a Gentile and a stranger in Israel, Ruth was an ancestor of the Messiah.

Ruth found her life, not in dwelling on her sorrow and loss in Moab, but in serving Naomi. It was through this loving service, this total giving of herself, that Ruth was so bountifully blessed.

Losses in our lives come in many shapes and sizes. A loss can be as monumental as the death of a child or spouse or parent. Or the loss may take the form of rejection through divorce or running away. The loss may be physical, such as blindness or the loss of a limb. Loss can include such everyday things as disap-

pointment in friends, destruction or loss of property or possessions, or missing out on a work opportunity. When these losses
occur, we cry out to God, asking him for comfort and for solutions. Often the comfort and the solutions come through other
people. The Lord holds us, soothes us, and loves us through the
arms and voices of our friends and loved ones. And the Lord
offers solutions and healing through our opportunities to serve
and love other people.

Jesus Christ gave completely of himself for us. "This is my
commandment, that you love one another as I have loved you.
Greater love has no man than this, that a man lay down his life
for his friends" (John 15:12-13).

*Dear Lord Jesus, sometimes our loss is so great that we can see
only inward, concentrating on our pain. Lord, lift our eyes to you
and your love. Give us comfort through family and friends. And
then give us the opportunity to love and serve other people.
Grant us peace and healing through service, Lord Jesus. Thank
you for giving your life that we may live with you eternally.*

To learn more about Ruth and about serving other people:
- Read the whole book of Ruth.
- Read John 15:1-17. Then make a point of calling a relative
  or friend who has recently experienced a loss of any kind.
  Volunteer to do something specific with and for that person.
- Are you suffering a painful loss? First read Matt. 11:28-30.
  Then call a person or an organization which is experiencing
  a need and offer to help. Make a specific commitment to do
  something—and then do it!

All Things Are Possible in the Lord!
Sarah

The Lord said to Abraham, "Why did Sarah laugh, and say, 'Shall I indeed bear a child, now that I am old?' Is anything too hard for the Lord? At the appointed time I will return to you, in the spring, and Sarah shall have a son." . . . And Sarah said, "God has made laughter for me; every one who hears shall laugh over me." And she said, "Who would have said to Abraham that Sarah would suckle children? Yet I have borne him a son in his old age." Gen. 18:13-14; 21:6-7

My husband's first parish was in western North Dakota, where he served three congregations and a Bible camp. His Sunday morning tour of the churches involved a journey of a hundred miles. Our car was a used station wagon, and one Sunday morning while Andy was driving to the third church, the engine literally fell out of it. He coasted into a farm yard belonging to a church member (thank you, Lord!) where a pickup truck always waited with the keys in the ignition just in case a hapless traveler needed it (thanks again, Lord!). He managed to get to the third church in time for the service, but our poor station wagon was in dreadful condition. A Monday morning diagnosis indicated that a rebuilt engine had to be installed. That engine would cost us $300. We did not have even a small percentage of that.

It was then that we began experiencing God's power in our impossible situation. The first demonstration, after a woman's funeral, involved an unusual gift which added $50 to the engine fund. Then came the emergency request for us to board a high school girl for four months at $50 per month. So far the payments on the engine were right on schedule! But the last $50 came from an unexpected source and to me seemed to demonstrate the Lord's sense of humor. The grocery store in Dickinson sponsored television bingo every week. Shoppers could collect as many game cards as they made trips to the store. I only had one card, but I turned the TV on just for the fun of it. The fun turned into amazement, then to disbelief, and then to hilarious rejoicing when I realized I had actually won $50. My one game card was the only winner that week. It was a miracle! Our engine was completely paid off and right on schedule. There are still people in North Dakota who remember the time their pastor's wife won bingo on television!

Our God is all-powerful. We often try to limit his power by thinking of God as being only like ourselves—human. But our God is God. All things are possible!

Sarah knew she was part of the great promise God had made to Abraham regarding descendants and a great nation. But years and years went by without any sign of children. It was very discouraging. Sarah tried to remedy the situation by offering her maid Hagar to Abraham, thinking that perhaps a child born to that union would be acceptable. Legally that child belonged to Sarah, since Hagar was her maid. But Ishmael was not the one God had in mind. And Sarah waited and waited. Finally God acted and Isaac was born. Never mind that Sarah was 90 and Abraham 100 years old. All things are possible for the Lord. Sarah said that God had made laughter for her.

One thing I've learned about my prayer life over the years is that I've tried to spare the Lord. I've often found myself not asking God for certain things because I felt it was asking too much or was too difficult or was even downright impossible. To my horror I've heard myself say, "Lord, if you are able. . . ." *If the Lord is able?* What am I saying! Of course of the Lord is able. He can do anything. He created the universe. Just because I can't comprehend such power and might, that doesn't limit God. I think that despite my human and sinful nature, I'm finally beginning to believe that God is all-powerful.

I now pray about anything and everything. Nothing is too large—nothing is too small. I've discovered a tremendous freedom in this kind of prayer. I used to censor my prayers; now I talk to the Lord about everything that concerns me.

After Isaac was born, Sarah had a different perspective of God's power and his will. After watching God at work in my life, I find that my trust level is at its highest point. I hear myself telling other people to pray about things, assuring them that I certainly will pray for them. I have great confidence in the Lord. Nothing is impossible for him.

Don't be afraid. Don't wonder if God is able to work miracles. Pray about everything, trusting God to care for your every need. "But Jesus looked at them and said to them, 'With men this is impossible, but with God all things are possible'" (Matt. 19:26).

Dear Lord God, we know that you are all-powerful but in our humanness we cannot comprehend such a wonder. Lord, help us grow in our prayers and in our trust so we may bring everything to you in complete confidence. And, Lord, thank you for loving us and caring for us even as we are caught in our sinful blindness and distrust. Today give us a special insight into your love and power.

To learn more about Sarah and also about God's power:
- Read Genesis 12; 15–17; 18:1-15; 21–23.
- Read Psalm 65; Rom. 1:16-17; 1 Cor. 1:18-25.
- A prayer list can help you discover God's power and faithfulness. Write down your petitions, dating each one. Pray over your requests to God. Then be sure to note the answer to each petition, dating it and thanking God for his love and mercy. Remember that a "no" or "wait a while" answer demonstrates God's love, because he knows exactly what is best for you.

Service Versus Manipulation
Rebekah

Rebekah said to her son Jacob, "I heard your father speak to your brother Esau, 'Bring me game, and prepare for me savory food, that I may eat it, and bless you before the Lord before I die.' Now therefore, my son, obey my word as I command you. Go to the flock, and fetch me two good kids, that I may prepare from them savory food for your father, such as he loves; and you shall bring it to your father to eat, so that he may bless you before he dies."   *Gen. 27:6-10*

At 17 Katie had a beautiful singing voice, rich and full. One day she and her singing partner, Jack, were delighted to be invited to participate in auditions for a famous movie producer. "It's the chance of a lifetime!" Katie told her parents. "Even if the movie producer doesn't like my work for this project, there's a chance he'll like it for something else!"

The upcoming auditions for Katie and Jack were the talk of the town. But Katie's parents were not happy. To their thinking, professional show business was evil and to be avoided. It was all right for Katie to sing in church and in school programs, but this was going too far. Katie would not be allowed to audition. Katie begged and wept and pleaded and bargained with her parents, but it was no use. They were convinced that Katie should give up the audition and go to college to prepare for something sensible.

Today many young people faced with this situation would run away from home, determined to pursue their own interests, but Katie lived when this almost never happened. So Katie was obedient, but her heart was rebellious. And the hurt and rebellion lived on in Katie for many years. It colored her attitude toward her family and her college work. Katie's whole life was affected by her parents' decision imposed upon her.

We can argue that Katie's parents were only acting in her best interests, and perhaps that was true. But it is also true that sometimes we become so convinced of our own opinions—even attributing them to God—that we impose our will on others, regardless of their feelings or desires.

Rebekah was convinced that her younger son Jacob should have his father's blessing. Rebekah loved Jacob. He was a quiet, introspective man while his twin brother Esau was an outdoor man, a hunter. When Rebekah saw the chance of tricking blind old Isaac into giving Esau's rightful blessing to Jacob, she immediately went to work. While Esau was out hunting the game which his father had requested, Rebekah prepared domestic meat and convinced Jacob to dress up like Esau. Even though Jacob protested that Isaac was bound to figure out the deception, Rebekah pursued her plan and helped Jacob carry it through. Sure enough, although he had a few doubts, Isaac finally believed the man in front of him was Esau and he gave the blessing: "Let peoples serve you, and nations bow down to you. Be lord over your brothers, and may your mother's sons bow down to you. Cursed be every one who curses you, and blessed be every one who blesses you!" (Gen. 27:29).

Once the blessing was given, it could not be taken away. When Esau hurried in a few moments later, Isaac could only cry out in sorrow and anger. Rebekah had succeeded in stealing the all-important blessing away from Esau for her favorite son.

The result of Rebekah's "success" in imposing her own will upon her family was tragic. Esau vowed to kill his brother, so Jacob had to leave in a hurry. Rebekah never saw her favorite son again. And she had to live with a husband who knew he had been deceived and with a son and his wives who knew they'd been cheated.

Yes, God's will was worked out even through the deception and tragedy. But the price in human sorrow, misery, hatred, and alienation was very great.

Our sinful natures often color our relationships with other people. It is only too natural for us to be convinced of our own points of view, refusing to listen to other people and criticizing their opinions or life-styles. Even when we believe we are serving the Lord, we can impose our own will on other people, hurting them and turning their hearts and lives away from us and—even worse—away from the Lord.

We must continually ask the Lord to temper our service with love and mercy. This can happen only if we are open to the Lord's guidance in Scripture and prayer, asking the Holy Spirit to demonstrate his love through us. This involves listening, caring, counseling, laughing, sharing, hugging, and even admitting error. God promises to work for good through all things among those who love him (Rom. 8:28). This includes the tragedies of life. But how wonderful when love and mercy allow communication and sharing. Who needs to have you listen—really listen—today?

Dear heavenly Father, so often we are convinced we have the right answers without even asking you or listening to other human beings. Show us how to demonstrate openness, love, and mercy in our relationships. Keep us, Lord from simply imposing our own ideas and our own will on others. Thank you, dear Father, for loving us so much that you sent your Son to earth to live, die, and rise again—right in our midst. Today give us the words and the love we need to minister rightly to others.

To learn more about Rebekah, as well as about loving service:
- Read Genesis 24; 25:19-34; 27:1—28:10.
- Carefully and slowly read 1 Corinthians 13. Note especially verses 4-7.
- Think about ways in which love will make a difference in how you treat people. Then thank God for loving us even though we are unlovable.

A Dedicated Life
Mary Magdalene

Soon afterward [Jesus] went on through cities and villages, preaching and bringing the good news of the kingdom of God. And the twelve were with him, and also some women who had been healed of evil spirits and infirmities: Mary, called Magdalene, from whom seven demons had gone out . . . and many others, who provided for them out of their means.   Luke 8:1-3

Mary Magdalene went and said to the disciples, "I have seen the Lord"; and she told them that he had said these things to her.
John 20:18

The change in my Uncle Ralph was incredible. He was suddenly turned around in his tracks by Christ. One day he was an unbeliever; the next day he knew his Lord. Ralph was a dentist in a small town in Minnesota and had been openly skeptical, even derogatory at times, about the church and Christianity. But a series of evangelistic services were held in the little town, and my aunt prevailed upon Ralph to attend. During those few days other people were given the spiritual gifts of speaking in tongues and of prophecy, but my uncle received the most important gift of all: faith and trust in Jesus Christ.

The change in Ralph was hard for my family to grasp. Now he read his Bible and books about faith with joy and zeal. He accepted an invitation to teach the high school Bible class. With eyes shining and a smile on his face, he told other people about his Lord. My uncle's favorite Bible personality was Paul, probably because their conversion experiences were so similar. Ralph lived on this earth for another six years. His gift of faith in Christ never faded but grew and grew. Our family has a precious memory of a man who was on fire for the Lord.

Mary Magdalene was a woman whose life also was turned completely around by her encounter with Jesus Christ. Although we don't know the nature of her illness or problem with the "seven demons," when she was healed, Mary gratefully dedicated her life to Jesus.

What is involved in living a life dedicated to the Lord? Perhaps we think of people in monasteries or cloisters as completely dedicated to God, believing that it's not possible to do when we're living ordinary lives. But Mary Magdalene, who lived in the real world, demonstrated true dedication and commitment in three specific aspects of her life:

Trust. After her healing, Mary trusted Jesus. She followed him to Golgotha and to the tomb, even when others had run away. Mary knew who had saved her, and she remembered Jesus' words and promises. Even in the face of death and destruction, Mary's faith and trust in her Savior were strong and unwavering.

Service. Mary's dedication was not limited to feelings and emotions. She followed Jesus as he traveled the country preaching, teaching, and healing. She gave her own money to help support the group. She stood vigil at the cross and anointed Jesus' body at the tomb. Mary noticed what was needed and did what she could.

Witness. Mary had good news to tell about Jesus' resurrection, and she was not shy about sharing it. Despite the disciples' disbelief, Mary insisted on the truth of what she knew about Jesus. She brought her witness with joy and enthusiasm.

It often seems that the person who has become a Christian later in life is filled with a special joy and enthusiasm. Perhaps it's a reaction to discovering how much has been missed in life and a desire to make sure that others will also share the joy of salvation. The Apostle Paul, converted on the road to Damascus, became a person on fire for Jesus. Mary Magdalene, healed of seven demons, poured out her life, her means, and her energies to Christ. My Uncle Ralph, touched by the fire of God's Spirit, became a beautiful, happy witness for his Lord.

Many people have believed in the Lord since they were children and have never known a time when they did not have faith in Christ. That, too, is a beautiful and precious gift. Their dedication to the Lord may not be quite as fiery and explosive as Paul's or Mary Magdalene's or my uncle's, but the qualities of dedication are the same: trust, service, witness.

Just as each one of us is a unique individual and as our gifts and experiences are different, so will these qualities be expressed in various ways in the body of Christ. That is beautiful! Every Christian, every gift, and every saving experience praises our Lord and Savior, Jesus Christ.

Dear Lord Jesus, you have healed us and saved us, lost and condemned sinners, by your life, death, and resurrection. Lord, we want our lives to be dedicated to you in every way. Help us trust you completely. Show us what tasks we may do in your kingdom. Give us a strong voice to tell others about your salvation. Dear Lord Jesus, use our special gifts and experiences to glorify your name and bring others to a realization of your love.

To learn more about Mary Magdalene, as well as about trust, service and witness:
- Read Luke 8:1-3; Matt. 27:45-61; John 20:1-18.
- Read 1 Peter 1:8-9; Eph. 2:8-9; 1 John 5:4-5.
- Read Phil. 2:1-4; Gal. 6:7-10; James 1:19-27; Amos 5:14-15, 24.
- Read Matt. 4:18-22; Acts 1:8; Luke 12:8-12; Heb. 12:1-2.
- Prayerfully examine your own Christian life. Where do you see evidences of trust? Of service? Of witness? Ask the Lord to give you grace to grow in each area.

Hardness of Heart
Drusilla and Bernice

After some days Felix came with his wife Drusilla, who was a Jewess; and he sent for Paul and heard him speak upon faith in Christ Jesus. And as he argued about justice and self-control and future judgment, Felix was alarmed and said, "Go away for the present; when I have an opportunity I will summon you."

Acts 24:24-25

So on the morrow Agrippa and Bernice came with great pomp, and they entered the audience hall with the military tribunes and the prominent men of the city. Then by command of Festus Paul was brought in. . . . [Paul said,] "King Agrippa, do you believe the prophets? I know that you believe." And Agrippa said to Paul, "In a short time you think to make me a Christian?"

Acts 25:23; 26:27-28

One look at the woman's face convinced me she was desperate. She had heard me teaching a Bible study on the work of the Holy Spirit. "I must talk to you," she said in a shaking voice. "Now!"

We found a quiet place to visit, and she poured out her sorrows and fears. "I am so terribly afraid of what I've done. I made life miserable for my husband while he was alive; I'm sure I brought about his death with my nagging. I just couldn't seem to help myself!" I hugged her and assured her of God's forgiveness.

But she refused to be comforted. "You don't know the whole story yet," she wept. "I'm so afraid—in fact, I'm certain—that I've committed the sin against the Holy Spirit!" And now the tears poured forth in earnest. She clung tightly to me. "Please tell me the truth," she begged. "I'm sure with all my problems and sins I've hardened my heart to the point where the Holy Spirit is rejected. I really am lost, aren't I?"

I had the opportunity to tell the woman the good news that she had not committed the sin she feared so much, but that the Holy Spirit was acting in her life even as we spoke. The very fact that she was so concerned was the best proof I had to show her that her heart was far from being hard.

When has the Holy Spirit been blasphemed? When is a heart hardened to the Holy Spirit? Blasphemy and hardness are present when the Spirit's calls are not only unheeded but are also unheard. No matter how long or insistently the Spirit may call, there is no response from the truly hardened heart.

Drusilla and Bernice were well on their way to hardened, blasphemous hearts. They and their brother King Agrippa were children of Herod Agrippa I (who murdered James, the apostle) and great-grandchildren of Herod the Great (who spoke to the Wise Men and slaughtered the baby boys in Bethlehem). They came from a long tradition of people who refused to listen to God.

The Apostle Paul had an opportunity to speak to each of the sisters. Drusilla was married to Governor Felix, who had Paul in prison in Caesarea. Drusilla listened one day as Paul spoke to her husband about justice, self-control, and judgment. Felix sent Paul away; what he really hoped for was a bribe.

Later Governor Festus tried to resolve the problem by bringing Paul before his guests, King Agrippa and Bernice, for a hearing. While speaking to the group, Paul explained his conversion to faith in Jesus Christ and challenged the king about his own beliefs. Privately Agrippa and Bernice agreed with Festus that Paul had done no wrong, but the king and Bernice left without truly listening to Paul's words about faith.

The term "hardness of heart" occurs frequently in the Bible. It refers to the obstinacy and rebellion of sinful human nature. In disbelief and pride, human nature desires to be in control, to determine the future. But God asks for first place in the human heart. "You shall have no other gods before me," said the Lord, and that includes the human will. And so the battle lines are drawn.

"Truly, I say to you, all sins will be forgiven the sons of men, and whatever blasphemies they utter; but whoever blasphemes against the Holy Spirit never has forgiveness, but is guilty of an eternal sin" (Mark 3:28-29). To blaspheme against the Holy Spirit is to reject and ignore his gracious call to faith. Since such rejection closes off the only possible avenue by which Christ's saving work can be given to the sinner, the obstinate, unrepentant person truly has committed an eternal sin. But the sorrowing, even doubting, human being is not blaspheming the Holy Spirit. He or she is responding to the Spirit's convicting call which is exposing the sins of rebellion and unbelief.

This is when prayer is desperately needed—prayer that God's Spirit will continue to work and that the person under conviction will receive God's grace with joy and gratitude. The prescriptions for any stage of a hardened heart are intercessory prayer, loving concern on the part of believers, and continued fellowship in the body of Christ, where the Word of God can continue its miracle of conversion and faith.

Dear Lord God, open our hearts and our minds to your Holy Spirit. Make us sensitive to your call and your love, to your teachings and guidance. Lord, help us to minister lovingly to those who are struggling in their faith. Give us patience, insight, and wisdom, as well as your perfect peace.

To learn more about Drusilla, Bernice, and Paul, and about the Holy Spirit's work:
- Read Acts 23:12—26:32. Then read John 14:15-31; Acts 2:1-42; Romans 8; Gal. 5:13-25.
- Be sure to exercise the practice of intercessory prayer for anyone experiencing hardness of heart or indifference to God's call. Also be sure to speak warmly and lovingly to anyone in these circumstances, for Jesus' sake.

Looking Forward, Not Backward
Lot's Wife

Then the Lord rained on Sodom and Gomorrah brimstone and fire from the Lord out of heaven; and he overthrew those cities, and all the valley, and all the inhabitants of the cities, and what grew on the ground. But Lot's wife behind him looked back, and she became a pillar of salt. Gen. 19:24-26

A feud in the family! For me as an idealistic teenager, it was hard to believe! But it was true. A certain woman in my family remembered very clearly what had been said and done to her by her husband's relatives during her engagement and shortly after her marriage. She made a point to explain to me in much detail what her mother-in-law had said, what her brother-in-law had said, and how it had all made her feel. To hear her tell it, all these things seemed to have happened last week. But actually they had happened nearly 30 years ago.

Gradually I began to realize that her feelings about the 30-year-old incidents colored her feelings and actions of the present day. Slights from years ago affected Christmas gifts and dinners today. Harsh words from years ago determined which roads were driven on present-day Sunday outings. Unkind actions from years ago generated gleeful vengeance in little ways today. Instead of being mellowed and healed by the years, the 30-year-old feud made life miserable for my relative and many people around her.

Lot's wife couldn't make up her mind whether she wanted the old life in Sodom or the new life which God had promised. Because of Abraham's intercession with God on behalf of his nephew, the Lord had promised to save Lot and his family. It wasn't easy getting Lot out of Sodom. God's angels had to seize Lot, his wife, and his two daughters by the hand and take them out of town to make them leave. And then when the family was finally outside the town, the angels gave these instructions: "Flee for your life; do not look back or stop anywhere in the valley; flee to the hills, lest you be consumed" (Gen. 19:17). The Lord rained brimstone and fire on the sinful cities of Sodom and Gomorrah, after saving Lot and his family in accordance with his promise to Abraham. But Lot's wife could not resist looking back on her old life, even though she had been specifically warned not to do so. She was punished for her disobedience in a grotesque yet suitable manner: she was turned into a pillar of salt, becoming part of the destroyed landscape.

We all do it. We all look backward in our lives, either wallowing in guilt and regret over our past sins or actively remembering past hurts inflicted upon us by others. Either way we are clinging to our history in a destructive fashion, allowing it to determine our feelings and activities in the present time. Individuals do this; families also do it; whole congregations can become embroiled in the activity of "looking back," either on past glories or past sins. Living in the past robs us of joy in the present and hope in the future.

The beautiful gift of Christ is the forgiveness of all our sins. This gift is meant to free us for joyful service. With God's love we are asked to forgive others and also to forgive ourselves. It is contrary to the beautiful freedom God gives us to hold grudges or continue to blame ourselves. We are new people in Christ!

How is such newness actually accomplished in day-to-day living? In *The Small Catechism* Martin Luther described the role of Baptism:

What does Baptism mean for daily living?

It means that our sinful self, with all its evil deeds and desires, should be drowned through daily repentance; and that day after day a new self should arise to live with God in righteousness and purity forever.

St. Paul writes in Romans 6:
"We were buried therefore with him by Baptism into death,

so that as Christ was raised from the dead by the glory of the Father, we too might walk in newness of life."

Daily washing in our baptismal covenant involves repentance as well as asking the Lord to give us new, clean hearts and spirits. This means that past failures and past injuries must be released to the Lord. We are not to cling to them and nurture them. Instead we can look joyously to the new day, to the eternal future we have with Jesus Christ.

What does your new, clean, fresh day hold in store for you? "Thanks be to God, who gives us the victory through our Lord Jesus Christ" (1 Cor. 15:57).

Dear Lord and Father, our necks are stiff from looking backward. Give us release from past sins and from remembered hurts, washing them away in the floods of your grace and mercy. Lord, help us to live each day in the newness and the freshness of your love, and show us how to share that love with our families, with everyone we meet today. Thank you for redeeming our lives through our Baptism into Christ's suffering, death, and resurrection. May we rise daily to worship and adore only you, O Lord.

To learn more about Lot and his family and also about Baptism:

- Read Gen. 13:2-13; 14:1-16; 18; 19; Luke 17:22-37; 2 Peter 2:4-10.
- Read Rom. 6:1-14; Eph. 4:1-6; Gal. 3:27.
- When the pastor makes the sign of the cross over the congregation, he or she is reminding the people of their baptismal covenant. The acts of crossing oneself and using holy water are also reminders of our Baptism. In terms of personal and family devotional activity, what are some ways in which we can "wash daily in our baptismal covenant"?
- Every time you use water today, remember your Baptism and thank God for washing your sins away for Jesus' sake.

Patience Is a Process
The Canaanite Woman

And behold, a Canaanite woman from that region came out and cried, "Have mercy on me, O Lord, Son of David; my daughter is severely possessed by a demon." But he did not answer her a word. And his disciples came and begged him, saying, "Send her away, for she is crying after us." . . . But she came and knelt before him, saying, "Lord, help me." . . . Then Jesus answered her, "O woman, great is your faith! Be it done for you as you desire." And her daughter was healed instantly. Matt. 15:22-28

The two years I lived in western North Dakota were filled with lessons in patience. One of these lessons was learned from Willie, a teenager afflicted with muscular dystrophy. Willie tried to deal with his progressively deteriorating body with determination and good humor. He occupied his time by writing poetry, studying the Bible, reading, visiting with family and friends. I can still see him sitting in his wheelchair in church, absorbing the music and Scripture. Every communion Sunday the ushers would lift Willie and his wheelchair up into the chancel so he, too, could be close to the altar, participating in the sacrament with the other people. Even in our short time in that parish, we could see Willie becoming weaker. He knew he was dying and often spoke of it. His poems reflected his strong belief in the Lord and the eternal life he knew was his. I was amazed at the patience in this young man and his parents. I could see it had developed over many years of coping with Willie's illness.

The Canaanite woman had learned patience through adversity, too. Her daughter was very ill. Undoubtedly the woman's life was spent caring for the girl and trying to find help for her. Jesus met the Gentile woman as he traveled to Tyre and Sidon, outside the land of the Jews. The woman knew about Jesus and begged him to help her: "Have mercy on me, O Lord, Son of David; my daughter is severely possessed by a demon." Then began the unusual exchange of words and ideas between Jesus and the Canaanite woman.

At first Jesus didn't answer her at all. Then, as she persisted, he spoke in picture language which, when interpreted, meant that he had come only to serve the Jews. But still the woman patiently persisted in her quest for help. "Yes, Lord, yet even the dogs eat the crumbs that fall from their master's table" (Matt. 15:27). She showed herself ready and willing to receive whatever Jesus would give her.

Finally Jesus was satisfied about the woman's intentions and he commended her: "O woman, great is your faith! Be it done for you as you desire." And the little girl was healed. The Canaanite woman had patiently persisted in her belief that Jesus was the answer for her desperate need.

Our best example of patience comes from God himself. The Old Testament is the story of God's patience with the Jewish people even when they worshiped other gods. His patience endured until, in his wisdom, God knew the time was right to send his only Son into the world to heal the brokenness of sin through his life, death, and resurrection.

We live in a world filled with impatience. Motorists honk at other motorists who aren't moving fast enough; parents shout at dawdling children; people pound and kick equipment that doesn't operate. We want things to happen for us and on our schedule. Impatience is really a way of expressing our frustration in not getting our own way.

Patience, on the other hand, is the product of love and unselfishness. It is characterized by calmness, persistence, and steadfastness even in the face of frustrations and delays. The Canaanite woman's daughter would not have been healed if her mother hadn't been steadfast and persistent on her behalf. And that patience most likely was acquired through her long experiences of caring for her sick daughter and of seeking help.

Patience is a beautiful gift from God. Paul lists it with other fruits of the Spirit in Galatians 5. But God does not inject us with "instant patience." Instead, like love, gentleness, and kindness, the gift of patience is given to us by a process which may involve many years and many wonderful and difficult experiences.

Ask the Lord for patience, but be aware that a long "patience-developing process" is necessary. One day you'll be amazed when someone says, "I wish I had your patience." You probably won't even realize that the gift has already been given.

Dear Lord and Holy Spirit, it is so hard for us to be patient even in little things. We pray for your love and mercy in helping us develop the gift of patience. Be with us in the difficulties and joys which are bound to come, using them to make us patient, loving people.

To learn more about the Canaanite woman, as well as about the gift of patience:

- Read Matt. 15:21-28; Mark 7:24-30.
- Read Luke 8:11-15; Rom. 8:18-25; Col. 3:12-15.
- Patience is closely linked with love. Write this verse on a card and put it up where you'll frequently see it: "Love is patient and kind" (1 Cor. 13:4).

Teaching the Faith
Eunice and Lois

I am reminded of your sincere faith, a faith that dwelt first in your grandmother Lois and your mother Eunice and now, I am sure, dwells in you. . . . But as for you, continue in what you have learned and have firmly believed, knowing from whom you learned it and how from childhood you have been acquainted with the sacred writings which are able to instruct you for salvation through faith in Christ Jesus.   2 Tim. 1:5; 3:14-15

Her name was Carrie, but it could just as well have been Eunice or Lois. Carrie taught the Bible stories to her little son Andrew, reading them to him long before he was able to read any words for himself—stories about Jesus, about Peter, about Abraham, about Joseph, about David, about Mary, about Ruth, about Paul. The Bible story books became ragged, but little hands could always find just the right page with the special story: "Here, mother! Read me this story!" Along with the stories, Carrie taught Andrew the truth about God's love in Jesus Christ, about the beautiful gift of salvation the child had received through his Baptism into Christ.

Carrie is dead now. Andrew became a pastor. People often say to him, "Pastor, you really know the Bible!" or "I've never known anyone who could make the Bible stories come alive like you do," or "Pastor, you seem so at home in the Scripture." And it's true. My husband knows and loves the Scriptures and is always hungry to read and learn more in them.

The Apostle Paul recognized faith, quality, and potential in young Timothy when he met him in Asia Minor during one of his missionary journeys. He asked Timothy to accompany him on his travels to spread the gospel of Jesus Christ. A picture is painted in 2 Timothy of the boy's influential home and upbringing. It was a home where the Scriptures had been opened to Timothy by his mother and grandmother. They taught Timothy the law, the prophets, and the poetic writings of what we know today as the Old Testament, steeping him in the stories and the truths. But Eunice, Timothy's mother, was a Christian (Acts 16:1) so she undoubtedly showed the boy how the Scriptures had been fulfilled in Jesus of Nazareth. Mother and grandmother taught him to love the Lord Jesus, the Messiah.

As an associate of Paul, Timothy visited congregations with words and messages from the apostle. Later Timothy became the pastor of the church in Ephesus. The two letters to Timothy are addressed to him there, containing counsel and advice on how to carry out pastoral duties. Eunice and Lois were in the background; it was Timothy who became the pastor and evangelist. But Paul was quick to see that the godly upbringing of Timothy by Eunice and Lois was the key to his strong Christian faith and his ability to share the gospel with other people.

Not surprisingly, considering his background of family Bible study and worship, my husband wrote his doctoral thesis on *Christian Education and Worship in the Home*. Based on a four-week family devotional experience in different types of homes, it became apparent that 1) children seem to learn from and absorb any material which their parents present to them; 2) children seem to receive these materials gladly and with enthusiasm; 3) children seem to learn and absorb ideas and knowledge even when their parents don't realize it is happening; and 4) children will sometimes reach out to try new things and experiences on their own even when the opportunities are only briefly presented. In other words, everything we teach our children is important; no effort is wasted.

What an encouragement this is to us as parents in our day of sophisticated tools such as television, satellites, and computers! Perhaps we have begun to feel that schools, media, and peer pressure are much more powerful influences than parents ever can be. We need to notice the two specific influences Paul mentions in regard to Timothy's home:

The faith of the parents and guardians is crucial. Parents who practice and confess their faith have great influence (2 Tim. 1:5).

The teaching and sharing of God's Word is imperative. The Word of God has power to convict of sin, to teach the way of salvation in Christ, and to open hearts and minds to God. Parents who use many opportunities to teach and explain God's Word are providing their child with a firm spiritual foundation (2 Tim. 3:14-15).

As parents we do not know what will become of our children. We are called to teach them the Christian gospel and pray that God will use their lives for his glory. Eunice and Lois must have spent many hours in prayer for Timothy, both when he was a child and after he left with Paul to begin his missionary work. Parents can support and uphold their children in prayer, believing and trusting that God "who began a good work in you will bring it to completion at the day of Jesus Christ" (Phil. 1:6).

Dear Lord Jesus, thank you for the gift of children in our lives. Give us the grace, the strength, and the patience to teach them the gospel message and to show by our words and our examples that you are also Lord in our lives. Jesus, our children belong to you, and we are your loving heart, arms, and voice for them on this earth. Draw us all closer to you, our Savior.

To learn more about Eunice, Lois, and Timothy, as well as about the power of God's Word:
- Read Acts 16:1-5; 17:1-15; 1 Cor. 4:17; 1 Thess. 3:1-10; Phil. 2:19-24.
- Read 1 and 2 Timothy, placing yourself in the shoes of the young pastor.
- Read Isa. 40:8; Ps. 119:103,105; Matt. 24:35; Rom. 10:14-17; Heb. 4:12.

The Individual Touch
The Woman Healed of the Hemorrhage

And Jesus, perceiving in himself that power had gone forth from him, immediately turned about in the crowd, and said, "Who touched my garments?" And his disciples said to him, "You see the crowd pressing around you, and yet you say, 'Who touched me?'" And he looked around to see who had done it. But the woman, knowing what had been done to her, came in fear and trembling and fell down before him, and told him the whole truth. And he said to her, "Daughter, your faith has made you well; go in peace and be healed of your disease."

Mark 5:30-34

When I was about 10 years old, my family lived in a small town in Wisconsin where we knew everyone and everyone knew us. Credit at the grocery store? Sure thing—we know you! Any mail for us? Let me check your box! Does anyone know where my little brother John is? Some neighbor was bound to have seen him in someone's yard. There was nothing in that comfortable, reassuring town of 850 people to prepare me for going to a New Jersey suburb of New York City when I was 15. Suddenly I was an unknown entity registering at a huge high school. Suddenly I was the only one in my class who was a Lutheran. It was even rare to find another Christian since the school was 85% Jewish. I had one special friend throughout high school, and together we managed to enjoy our teens in the big city.

Now I live in Los Angeles where the freeway system is marvelous but the mass of humanity traveling in cars, vans, trucks, and motorcycles is mind-boggling. Day and night there are people whizzing by on their way to somewhere and anywhere. In the impersonal world of this megalopolis and its freeways many people choose to single themselves out with a personalized license plate. We are no exception! Our station wagon now sports the license MYT 4TRS (Mighty Fortress) and the red car carries NORVGIN (Norwegian, with an accent!). Even though we know that only a few people will interpret our Lutheran and Norwegian codes, we enjoy being different, standing out in this big, big crowd even in a small way.

The woman had suffered with a flow of menstrual blood for 12 years. Not only was this an uncomfortable and debilitating problem, but it made her "unclean" as far as the religious laws were concerned. Everything she touched and sat on automatically became unclean. She spent her life trying to find a cure, as well as trying not to cause other people problems with her uncleanness.

The crowd was large around Jesus. Undoubtedly the woman believed she would not bother him by touching his garment—after all, with all these people around him he wouldn't even know she was there. *Careful—easy now—just reach out and touch Jesus' garment.* And her dream became reality. She was healed! Now—she could just slip back into the crowd and wouldn't even be noticed.

But Jesus did notice the woman. Even in the crush of humanity about him he knew she was there and had reached out to him. Even the disciples were amazed. How could Jesus possibly single out one individual in this crowd? Jesus spent a few moments talking to the frightened woman who hadn't wanted to bother anyone. "Daughter, your faith has made you well; go in peace, and be healed of your disease." Imagine the relief and the joy! Not only was her uncleanness gone and her disease healed, but the Lord had spoken personally to her, understanding her fears and her problems. Jesus had sought her out. He had cared about *her*. Today we don't even know her name.

God knows you deeply, personally, and completely. He knows you better than you know yourself. Think of the very best friend you ever had. Think of your parents at their most loving. Think of the person who cares the most for you in all the world. That's what God is like, and much, much more! That means that he hears every word you say and understands why you say it. He wants only good for you and will work through even the bad things to show you his love. He answers all your prayers according to what he knows to be the very best for you. Like a loving parent, he won't always give you what you want but will always act in your best interest.

Knowing all this about God, we also know that we can trust him completely. We can pray to him in joy and sorrow, in petition and praise, in peace and in problems. In joyous faith and love we can claim every one of the promises he has made to us. We are not mere numbers or atoms or paperdoll figures to our Lord and Savior. He loved us so deeply that he came to earth to be like us and to die on the cross for us. And he offers us eternal life with him in this utterly personal and loving relationship. That eternal life begins right here and right now.

Dear Lord Jesus, we are astounded to realize that you know and love each and every one of us. Thank you for being our personal Savior and Lord. Thank you for being our perfect friend and for listening to every word we think or say. Help us, Lord Jesus, to recognize our own worth in your eyes, knowing that you lived and died and rose again—for US! Today we ask a special measure of your love, joy, and peace in our lives. Touch us and make us completely yours.

To learn more about the woman who was healed, as well as about our personal Lord:
- Read Mark 5:21-43. Note the story within a story. Even while involved in another problem, Jesus noticed the woman. Also note Luke 8:40-56; Matt. 9:18-26.
- Note Jesus' personal approach in Luke 23:39-43; Matt. 4:18-22; 14:22-36; 15:21-28; 19:13-15; 20:29-34; 26:6-13; Luke 22:47-51.
- What difference will it make in your prayer life when you regard God as even more loving and caring than your best friend in all the world?

Faith Results in Works
Rahab

Then the king of Jericho sent to Rahab, saying, "Bring forth the men that have come to you, who entered your house; for they have come to search out all the land." . . . But she had brought them up to the roof, and hid them with the stalks of flax which she had laid in order on the roof. . . . Then she let them down by a rope through the window, for her house was built into the city wall, so that she dwelt in the wall.

Josh. 2:3, 6, 15

And in the same way was not also Rahab the harlot justified by works when she received the messengers and sent them out another way? For as the body apart from the spirit is dead, so faith apart from works is dead.   James 2:25-26

As I walk around our neighborhood in Los Angeles, I see fruit trees laden down with ripe oranges, grapefruit, tangerines, or lemons. Last year our family bought two varieties of dwarf orange trees and planted them in large wooden tubs on our patio. We wanted to see for ourselves how an orange tree produces its fruit. First there were new shoots of branches and leaves; after a few months we noticed little white blossoms beginning to form. Now they are at the point of blossoming out, and already the sweet fragrance is apparent. Some of these blossoms are going to turn into oranges. We can't wait to see our little trees producing fruit!

When I visited a friend recently I noticed that a huge tree in her front yard had many, many blossoms on it. On closer inspection I could see the blossoms matched the ones on my dwarf orange trees. Already the signs of the coming fruit were visible on both the dwarf tree and the full-grown tree. They were both doing what they were meant to do—produce oranges.

When we bought our orange trees, we expected them to produce fruit. If, after a season or two, we had seen no sign of blossoms or fruit we would have been very unhappy. We would have wondered if these trees were healthy. Perhaps we would have wondered if these actually were orange trees. It is, after all, by the fruit of the tree that we recognize its identity.

Jesus said, "I am the vine, you are the branches. He who abides in me, and I in him, he it is that bears much fruit, for apart from me you can do nothing" (John 15:5).

Rahab lived in Jericho when the children of Israel were conquering the land of Palestine. Two Hebrew spies came to her home (which some have called an inn) and lodged there. The king of Jericho heard about the two men and demanded that Rahab turn them over to him. But she protected the men, hiding them on the rooftop under stalks of flax, telling the king that the men already had left the city. Soon the king had sent soldiers to pursue the spies.

Rahab knew she was doing a dangerous thing. But she explained to the spies that she believed in the Lord of Israel. The people had heard about the mighty works of the Lord, Rahab said, "and as soon as we heard it, our hearts melted, and there was no courage left in any man, because of you; for the Lord your God is he who is God in heaven above and on earth beneath" (Josh. 2:11). Rahab's faith in the Lord of Israel gave her courage and confidence to help the Hebrew spies. She showed them how to escape through a window in her house, which was built into the city wall. The men let themselves down on a rope. But before they left, they promised Rahab that she and her family would be saved during the siege of Jericho.

The Letter to the Hebrews praises Rahab's faith, but James points out that her works on behalf of the spies were a result of her faith. James then goes on to teach that faith without works is dead. That sounds very harsh, but it's clear in Jesus' teachings that he expected his disciples to respond with good works: "You did not choose me, but I chose you and appointed you that you should go and bear fruit and that your fruit should abide" (John 15:16).

We see these fruits of faith in Christians around us. Ralph and Linda bring fresh bread and canned goods for the man at church who is hungry. Jan writes encouraging notes to people who are sorrowing or are disappointed, to people who are working hard or celebrating a happy occasion. Doris can always find time to give a ride to another child or be the sponsor of another school event. Roy never fails to give hugs and loving words to lonely, searching youngsters.

God has given us the beautiful gift of faith. We do not earn either our salvation or our faith, but God's Spirit enables us to act out our faith in loving, caring, merciful ways, bearing much fruit.

Dear Lord Jesus, you have chosen us to be your disciples, as you choose all who believe in you. You have appointed us to bear much fruit, serving our fellow human beings. Today, Lord, grant us the opportunities to love people for your sake; show us ways to tell others about your wondrous mercy; give us the courage and strength to be servants of one another. And, Lord Jesus, fill us with peace and joy in our serving.

To learn more about Rahab, as well as about faith and works:
- Read Joshua 2; 6:1-25; Heb. 11:29-31; James 2:18-26.
- Read Matt. 7:15-20; Luke 6:43-45; John 15:1-17.
- We are not to judge other people; we are only to judge ourselves. Ask the Lord's insight, wisdom, and grace to examine your life: "Am I bearing fruit in response to God's love and mercy? Is my faith reflected in my life? What can I do to share God's grace with others?" Then ask the Lord Jesus to fill you with his love and show you how to serve him.

Growth in Faith
Salome

And [Jesus] said to [Salome], "What do you want?" She said to him, "Command that these two sons of mine may sit, one at your right hand and one at your left, in your kingdom."

Matt. 20:21

And when the sabbath was past, Mary Magdalene, and Mary the mother of James, and Salome, brought spices, so that they might go and anoint him. And very early on the first day of the week they went to the tomb when the sun had risen.

Mark 16:1-2

The birth announcement just arrived! Jesse Clark Friedlein was born on May 22. Steve and Debbie are enjoying the wonder of new life given to them by God.

The new parents are not planning to feed Jesse roast beef and apple pie next week. They will not expect him to run the 50-yard dash or to explain his needs in carefully articulated sentences. Jesse is a newborn. Steve and Debbie will treat him as such, watching him grow and develop, always challenging him but not expecting more than Jesse can deliver at his stage of development. Ten years from now Jesse will be able to run, speak, and eat, but even then he'll need guidance and direction until he's fully developed—physically, emotionally, and mentally.

Every one of us begins our life with Jesus as a newborn, whether we are brought in Baptism as an infant or whether we come to faith as an adult. We are babies in our spiritual lives and are fed on "milk," not on "solid food" at the beginning (Heb. 5:12-14).

Salome, her sons James and John, and all of the people following Jesus were young in their relationship with the Lord. They had not yet come to understand the full purposes of Jesus' life and teachings. One day Salome came to Jesus and requested that her two sons be allowed to sit at Jesus' right and left hands in his kingdom. In her limited understanding, Salome—and the disciples, too—believed that Jesus' kingdom would be of this world, that he would be a king who controlled land, politics, and people. These "infants in the faith" did not yet realize that Jesus' kingdom was a spiritual one and that he would die for the sins of the world, being raised from death to conquer sin, death, and the devil for all time.

Jesus did not throw Salome out of his presence. Instead, he was firm in telling her and her sons that much pain and sorrow would come and that his kingdom would be different from what they anticipated. One might expect Salome to leave the group, disappointed, disheartened, and perhaps even angry. But even though we do not hear any more about Salome during Jesus' ministry, she is very much present at both the crucifixion and the empty tomb (Matt. 27:55-56; Mark 15:40-41; 16:1). She had not left Jesus but had continued in faith, even to the foot of the cross. What a marvelous surprise awaited Salome and the other women on the first day of the week! And through it all, Salome's faith was growing, developing, and maturing.

The church calls growth in faith "sanctification." The word itself means "becoming holy or pure." Infants in the faith—mature Christians, too—are fed through worship, study of the Scripture, prayer, fellowship with other believers, and service to the Lord. Growth, development, and maturity do not occur overnight; they are parts of a long and gradual process. People who are young in the faith need to realize that growth and understanding will come. People who are mature in the faith need to be patient with the "infants," helping them learn, understand, and grow.

For Christians life on earth is really a school which is preparing us for our life with God forever. How anxious we should be to know his Word, to communicate with him in prayer, to worship him at every opportunity! How important it should be to us to share the good news with other people, to help them grow and develop in faith! How delighted we should be at every new Baptism, every confession of faith, every new understanding! And how willing we should be to serve in God's kingdom here on earth, knowing that now we are only standing in the wings of the beautiful and everlasting drama God is unfolding in his glorious and perfect will for all who believe in Christ.

Dear Lord and heavenly Father, you have created us and you sustain us from day to day. You have given us faith and you help us grow in it daily. Through your Holy Spirit draw us to worship, to read your Word, to pray, to fellowship with other believers. Sanctify us, Lord, in your truth and grace.

To learn more about Salome and her sons, as well as about growth in faith:

- Read Matt. 4:18-22; 20:17-28; Mark 10:35-45; Matt. 27:45-56; Mark 15:33-41; 16:1-8; Acts 3:1—4:31; 12:1-2.
- Think about other Bible people who grew in faith. Read about Peter in the Gospels and about Paul in Acts. Remember that the beautiful letter of 1 John was written by John the apostle.
- Examine your own spiritual life. In what ways are *you* growing and maturing?

Praise God with Me!
Miriam

Then Miriam, the prophetess, the sister of Aaron, took a timbrel in her hand; and all the women went out after her with timbrels and dancing. And Miriam sang to them: "Sing to the Lord, for he has triumphed gloriously; the horse and his rider he has thrown into the sea." Exod. 15:20-21

A woman stood on my doorstep, her face beaming with joy. "My son has awakened from his coma! He's talking to us and he's begun to eat. Praise God! My son is going to be well." I praised the Lord with her.

As believers in the Lord we share with each other our experiences which demonstrate God's power, love, grace, and mercy. We praise God for his great deeds and urge others to praise and worship the Lord with us.

The Hebrew people had just crossed the parted Red Sea on dry land. The Egyptian soldiers in their chariots and on their horses were in hot pursuit. The thousands and thousands of Hebrews looked back at Pharaoh's army, and their hearts pounded in fear and dread. Then the waters of the sea poured back, drowning the soldiers and the horses while the Hebrews sang and danced for joy on the far shore. They were free! God had saved them.

Miriam, the sister of Moses and Aaron, led the celebration. The women followed her example, dancing and shaking timbrels. The song Miriam sang is one of the oldest pieces of recorded Hebrew poetry:

Sing to the Lord, for he has triumphed gloriously;

The horse and his rider he has thrown into the sea.

The glory belonged to the Lord! It was by God's hand that the

Hebrew slaves were now free. They were free to be God's people and to worship in word and deed.

My aunt walked carefully with her cane, holding on to my hand. "God has taken such good care of me!" she exclaimed. "I'm so happy when I think of how he has provided for me. I know he'll open the next door, too." I, too, thanked the Lord and expressed my confidence in him.

The psalmist sang, "Make a joyful noise to the Lord, all the lands! Serve the Lord with gladness! . . . For the Lord is good; his steadfast love endures for ever, and his faithfulness to all generations!" (Ps. 100:1, 5).

Paul wrote to the Philippians, "Rejoice in the Lord always; again I will say, Rejoice. Let all men know your forbearance. The Lord is at hand" (Phil. 4:4-5).

We can find many opportunities to tell others about God's great deeds. This sharing may be at a special time when the Lord's activity is highly visible, as for Miriam or the woman whose son was recovering. This sharing may occur during times of fear or sorrow, when we hold each other closely and recall God's past mercies, expressing our hope and confidence in God's faithfulness. This sharing may happen very naturally during daily activities, when we tell our children, our co-workers, or our friends about God's power and presence in our lives.

God uses our voices to tell the world about his love, his power, and his faithfulness. He uses our enthusiasm and our trust to lead others to praise him.

A pastor led the ceremonies at a retirement dinner for a beloved church worker in Los Angeles. "I praise God for the life and the work of this special man. Let everyone here say 'Amen!'" With the crowd of people I shouted, *"Amen!"*

Today is a special opportunity to praise the Lord in both word and deed! Share God's power, grace, and love with your family, especially with your children; your co-workers, in a professional or a volunteer situation; fellow believers in Christ, as well as those who are outside the church; anyone who may cross your path today.

Dear Lord and Father, you have poured out your love, your grace, your mercy, and your power upon us in so many ways. Open our hearts and our lips in your praise today. Give us a special opportunity to share with others what you have done for us. And Lord, give us joyful, thankful hearts out of which to proclaim your great love in our lives.

To learn more about Miriam and the praise of God:
- Read Exod. 2:1-10; 15:19-21.
- Read Num. 12:1-16; 20:1; 26-59; Micah 6:4.
- Scan the psalms. Note how many psalms encourage people to praise God. Memorize a "praise passage" which is especially meaningful to you.

Lord, Use My Life to Your Glory!
Mary of Nazareth

And Mary said, "Behold, I am the handmaid of the Lord; let it be to me according to your word." And the angel departed from her.   Luke 1:38

My mother and I had a standing joke based on an old television commercial. In it a young woman was trying to do a task and her mother was giving unsolicited assistance. Finally the young woman said with great exasperation, *"Please, mother! I'd rather do it myself!"* This statement became a humorous yet meaningful communication code in the relationship I had with my mother. I was trying to grow up, to become independent. My mother was eager to give me all her accumulated wisdom and experience. Fortunately we were usually comfortable with each other, and the commercial line gave an occasional tense situation just the humorous perspective it needed.

Human beings like to be independent, "to stand on their own two feet." That's healthy, because we are capable of doing and being so many things in our lives. But our sinful nature would have us believe that we also need to be independent of God. Indeed, the sin of Adam and Eve was that they tried to be like God instead of being satisfied with their "creature" status.

Today the word *submission* has ugly connotations for women who are trying to establish independence and freedom in relationships and careers. Human beings of either sex and in any century have never liked the idea of submission, because it means a loss of independence. And, of course, we all want to be free.

My father tells about a kite that wanted to be free. It sailed in the air, enjoying the dips and dives and then the new heights to which it soared in the wind currents. Eventually the kite tired of being confined to one area and tried to sail away, but the

72

string held it firmly in place. "Oh, if only I could be free of this string!" the kite thought. "Then I'd be free to go anywhere and I could sail to new, unheard-of heights." So the kite tugged and pulled on the string. Finally, with great effort, the kite broke away, and sure enough—it sailed higher and higher, further and further away from the old location. After a while the kite began to notice that it couldn't sail any higher. Not only that, the kite was losing altitude quickly. Oh, yes, there'd be occasional spurts of height and velocity, but they were short-lived. Gradually the kite sank lower and lower; finally it lay flat on the ground. Try as it would, the kite could not get up, let alone fly. And there the kite came to its understanding: the thing which the kite had believed held it down was the very thing which kept it in the air. The kite had true freedom only when it was held securely by the string.

Mary of Nazareth probably was a teenager when the angel Gabriel appeared to her. Here was a young girl with her whole life ahead of her. She was betrothed to Joseph, and undoubtedly the couple had made special plans together. Gabriel's appearance and message suddenly changed Mary's life: "Do not be afraid, Mary, for you have found favor with God. And behold, you will conceive in your womb and bear a son, and you shall call his name Jesus. He will be great, and will be called the Son of the Most High . . . and he will reign over the house of Jacob for ever; and of his kingdom there will be no end" (Luke 1:30-33).

Mary's response is startling. Yes, she had questions—"How can this be?"—but in response to God's earth-shattering announcement Mary was submissive and humble: "Behold, I am the handmaid of the Lord; let it be to me according to your word."

To be submissive to God is to give him our lives. The Lord created each one of us and knows us completely. It is only through him that we become what we are intended to be. Apart from God we can do nothing. Yet through our sinful nature the devil tries to convince us that God will only hold us down and that we are free only if we can break away. *"Please,* God! I'd

73

rather do it *myself!* Submissive? No way! I've got to be free, and I've got to be me!"

Like the kite, however, we find only problems and eventual failure by trying to be free from the very thing which holds us up. It is not God's intention to force us into submissive slavery in order to show his power and demonstrate that we are under his heel. No, he loves his creation and is delighted to have us do, and be, and accomplish. Submission to God does not hold us down, but it frees us for larger living.

Mary of Nazareth submitted herself to God, becoming his "handmaid." This beautiful submission and surrender of her life resulted in the joy and glory of being the mother of the Savior. Mary's life was used by God to his glory and for the salvation of all people.

The Lord knows you completely. After all, he created you. Your greatest freedom will come when your life, your attitudes, and your capabilities are completely given to him. Then your life will glorify God and will be everything God meant it to be.

Dear Lord God, you have created us, and you continue to sustain us even when we turn away. You loved us so much you sent Jesus to be our Savior. Lord, use our lives for your glory and help us to be all you want us to be. Take away our fears, our doubts, our confusion. Keep us completely in your love and in your will.

To learn more about Mary of Nazareth, as well as about freedom in Christ:
- Read Luke 1:26-56; 2:1-52; Matt. 12:46-50; John 19:25-27; Acts 1:12-14; 2:1-4.
- Read 2 Cor. 3:17-18; Gal. 5:1, 13; John 8:31-36.
- It's a paradox. Think deeply about this statement: "Complete submission to God can make me completely free." Talk it over with a Christian friend.

The Proverbial Mirror
The Virtuous Woman in Proverbs 31

Strength and dignity are her clothing, and she laughs at the time to come. She opens her mouth with wisdom, and the teaching of kindness is on her tongue. She looks well to the ways of her household, and does not eat the bread of idleness.   Prov. 31:25-27

Mirrors are fascinating to little children. They touch their image, wondering and laughing. My boys used to kiss their image, then laugh at the silly boy in the mirror.

Adults are fascinated by mirrors, too. We tend to check ourselves out in large store windows as we pass by; we study ourselves carefully in the bathroom mirror to see if blemishes or gray hairs have appeared since the last time we checked.

Mirrors can distort our image. Fun-house mirrors turn us into pear-shaped oddities or hideous monsters. Magnifying mirrors show up every pore and broken capillary. Cracked mirrors make us look divided and off-center. Dirty mirrors give us spots and wrinkles we don't deserve. Perhaps we dream about mirrors that would show us to be beautiful, trim, and perfectly groomed. The witch in "Snow White" wanted her mirror to assure her of her incomparable beauty.

But good mirrors give us the straight story. There we can discover if we've combed our hair properly, if the makeup is applied becomingly, if the clothes are fitting the way they should. The mirror faithfully reflects us the way we are.

Proverbs 31:10-31 tells about the "virtuous woman." These verses are filled with descriptions of a woman who does wonderful things. She is a good wife to her husband; she provides food for her household; she keeps the lamp lighted; she helps the poor and needy; she's an efficient homemaker and a good business-woman; she's a teacher of wisdom and of kindness; she's not lazy; her children and her husband praise her and respect her; her faith in the Lord is seen as her greatest attribute.

At first glance this "virtuous woman" seems unbearable. How can she be Mrs. Perfect? And who would even like her if she were? Doesn't she ever get tired? Isn't she ever discouraged?

Actually, this portrait of a God-fearing, faithful woman is not meant to be a threat but a mirror, a reflection by which we can see ourselves, by which we can learn and grow.

For example: note that the verses are filled with action words. The woman seeks, provides, perceives, reaches out, makes, sells, delivers, laughs. She's a *doing* person. These verbs describe a wife and mother as well as a career woman. The verbs show a person who is concerned for others as well as herself.

Then note the variety of activities in which the woman is involved. She is a woman who cares well for her household, who is a shrewd businesswoman, who helps the unfortunate, who loves her family. This is no one-dimensional, undeveloped, self-centered person. She is educated, interested in others, curious, courageous. All these things make her an interesting person.

Finally, note the source of her strength and vitality. She is a woman who fears the Lord. Her attitudes and motives are high and pure because her trust and faith is in God, not in herself or in her family. Her life is lived in response to the grace of God.

This virtuous woman is not to be feared, ridiculed, or avoided. She provides a beautiful, gracious mirror for our study and emulation.

Let's see: what can I learn about inner characteristics? Verse 25 says, "Strength and dignity are her clothing, and she laughs at the time to come." What does that mean to me in the latter part of the 20th century, in the days of women's rights and freedoms? It's a description of self-confidence, an assurance of the worth of my God-given talents, gifts, and capabilities. I am not put down by others; neither am I better than others. My trust is in the Lord, so I can live joyously day to day instead of worrying about the future. I, too, can "laugh at the time to come." That's a beautiful attitude of trust and faith.

Looking again into the mirror, what can I learn about family relationships? Verse 27 says, "She looks well to the ways of her household, and does not eat the bread of idleness." That doesn't make of me a household slave; rather it assures me that caring for a husband, for children, for other people in a home is a beautiful and worthwhile calling; it's worth doing well. Verse 28 assures me that those in my care will realize that I loved them so much I gave them the very best efforts I had.

Proverbs 31 is a beautiful, perfect mirror. It doesn't distort; it doesn't unduly magnify; it doesn't create an ugly reflection. It's worth my careful study and examination. As my son Joel would say, "Looking good, Mom! Looking good!"

Dear Lord, thank you for creating me a woman. Thank you for giving me the opportunities to serve my loved ones, my friends, my fellow workers—for your sake. But I get tired, Lord, and I get discouraged. Give me the rest and peace I need to continue my loving, to continue my important work.

To learn more about the "ideal woman" and about your own reflection:
- Read Prov. 31:10-31.
- First write down all the verbs. Then write down the descriptions of this woman's character and actions. Think carefully about your own life, work, and opportunities. What encouragement do you receive from Proverbs 31 today?

No Gift Is Too Small
The Maid of Naaman's Wife

Now the Syrians on one of their raids had carried off a little maid from the land of Israel, and she waited on Naaman's wife. She said to her mistress, "Would that my lord were with the prophet who is in Samaria! He would cure him of his leprosy." . . . So Naaman went down and dipped himself seven times in the Jordan, according to the word of the man of God; and his flesh was restored like the flesh of a little child, and he was clean.

2 Kings 5:2-3, 14

A beautiful memory quilt hangs in our front hall. I see it many times each day and am reminded of the love of a former parish. Sixty-five women and two men contributed their efforts in creating the quilt which tells about our six years in Burnsville, Minnesota. The little details on the quilt are striking: on the map of Minnesota appear tiny sugar beets, stalks of corn, a canoe, Paul Bunyan and a mosquito; a miniature red mailbox (with flag!) is found on the square containing our house; delicate rainbow rays flash from a prism on the Bethel Bible Study scroll; little musical notes dance over the heads of two of our boys as they play their instruments; the detailed Luther rose is carefully needlepointed on the square depicting the anniversary of the Augsburg Confession; the chancel cross of the church, given in memory of my mother, is depicted in the center of the quilt. The one-of-a-kind memory quilt is a composite of little details made by individuals contributing their gifts to the whole project. Some people sewed only a few stitches; others worked on the total design. But each contribution was important, and the total result is glorious!

The girl had been taken forcibly from her home in Israel by the Syrian army on one of its raids. She was made a slave in the house of Naaman, the commander of the Syrian army, and waited on Naaman's wife. Naaman suffered from leprosy, but it must have been a type of leprosy which was not contagious since he was not isolated from his people. No matter what the skin disorder was, it was a big problem to Naaman, who probably had tried many types of cures. The Israelite maid, having compassion on her master, spoke up with a suggestion: the prophet Elisha in Samaria cured people of leprosy. Naaman should go to him.

Probably the most amazing aspect of this whole story is that everyone took the little slave girl's word seriously. We might expect apathy or even derision at any suggestion a foreign slave girl would make, but that didn't happen. The little maid told Naaman's wife about Elisha, who told her husband, who told the king of Syria. The king, in turn, wrote a letter to the king of Israel, commending Naaman to him and sending along 10 talents of silver, 6000 shekels of gold, and 10 festal garments. This was a king's treasure sent as payment for a cure for Naaman, all based on the words of a little slave girl.

We easily talk about tiny mustard seeds and little acorns, pointing out the tremendous results in mustard bushes and oak trees. But we don't transfer that idea to ourselves very well. Instead we tend to downgrade our own talents, gifts, and opportunities. "I'm nobody," we might say, or "I really don't have any talent at all," or "What *I* do doesn't count for anything."

The Apostle Paul emphasized the picture of the body of Christ. Each believer has been gifted by the Holy Spirit to benefit the whole body. Every gift is important. We all have a unique contribution to make. No one gift will accomplish the entire task. It's the nature of the body of Christ to require many types of activities and talents. But if we downgrade our particular gift, not seeing it as worthy or important, we are depriving the body of a necessary aspect of its health and growth. Paul taught that we are to be humble but that we are to contribute what we are able.

When Naaman finally made contact with Elisha and obeyed

the command to wash in the Jordan River, he was healed. The little maid's words to her mistress resulted in the healing, joy, and gratitude of the important Syrian commander. They also led him to believe in and worship the God of Israel.

When we use our abilities and opportunities in Jesus' name, we are contributing to God's beautiful and effective will and purpose. The telephone call to a hurting friend, the trip to the market for an ailing neighbor, the soothing of a child's grief, the sharing of a spouse's frustration, the cleaning of a home or a church, the typing of a letter or flyer—no one thing seems that big or that important. But it is. Every stitch on our quilt is important; every word the little maid spoke to her mistress counted; every word and deed of love travels far; every contribution of talent, energy, or treasure to the body of Christ is vital.

What is your gift? What can you share today? Remember that in everything God gives the growth and the miracle.

Dear Lord God, we often feel insignificant and unimportant in this world. We tend to compare ourselves to others and believe that our talents and our efforts don't count for much. Today, Lord, infuse us with your power and your grace, allowing us to see what we may do to be the body of Christ in this world. May we be your arms and legs, your voice and your smile to your people, Lord. Give us joy and confidence in your service.

To learn more about Naaman and the little maid, as well as about the importance of all gifts:
- Read 2 Kings 5. Note all the results of the little maid's words.
- Read 1 Corinthians 12 and 13. What is the most important gift? Think about ways you can implement this gift in your home, in your work, in your church.

Persistence in Prayer
The Shunammite Woman

So she set out, and came to the man of God at Mount Carmel. When the man of God saw her coming, he said to Gehazi his servant, "Look, yonder is the Shunammite; run at once to meet her, and say to her, Is it well with you? Is it well with your husband? Is it well with the child?" And she answered, "It is well." And when she came to the mountain to the man of God, she caught hold of his feet. And Gehazi came to thrust her away. But the man of God said, "Let her alone, for she is in bitter distress; and the Lord has hidden it from me, and has not told me."   2 Kings 4:25-27

Human beings thrive on a routine. Vacations are great, surprises are fun, spur-of-the-moment jaunts are delightful, but in the long run we usually find that a steady routine makes us happy and productive.

Item 1: Day in and day out we prepare meals and we eat them, because we need nourishment to survive. Food and eating could become very boring, even sickening, if it weren't for our wonderful variety of foods. I'm convinced God has provided us with this fantastic variety as well as the knowledge of how to prepare them in so many ways because 1) eating is essential to our survival, 2) we need variety to maintain interest in the food which nourishes us, and 3) God wants us to enjoy this essential, even mundane activity.

Item 2: Maintaining a garden and a lawn in California is highly dependent on frequent watering. It took me a year to figure out the proper schedule of watering the flowers and plants in our patio. Now that I have an effective routine of frequent watering, the camellias, azaleas, begonias, coleus, cyclamen, and impatiens are doing very well.

Item 3: Nathan, my 15-year-old son, practices the piano faithfully and willingly. He has a natural talent for music, and it's not unusual for him to rehearse up to two hours every day. This immersion in the art of piano playing is paying handsome dividends. Not only does Nathan perform beautifully, but he now composes his own music. He receives great joy from classical music, is very knowledgeable on the subject, and will talk about it to anyone who will listen.

All of these activities involve persistence: persistence in eating, in watering, in rehearsing. And they all result in strength and well-being.

The Shunammite woman was persistent, too. She knew the prophet Elisha could help her, and she wouldn't accept anyone else. The woman from Shunem had known the prophet a long time, having given him food and water and even a special room in which to rest when he came through town. Elisha, grateful for her help, promised a special blessing of the Lord upon the childless woman—a son.

When the child was grown, perhaps 10 years old, he suffered a sunstroke and a few hours later died in his mother's arms. Instead of wailing helplessly, the woman carefully laid the boy on the bed in the prophet's resting room, called for a servant and a donkey, and rode to Mount Carmel to find Elisha. This was a journey of 20 miles, but the Shunammite woman was determined to get Elisha to help her son, even though she knew the boy was already dead. On she rode, the hot sun blazing down on her.

When she finally found Elisha, she fell at his feet and clung to them. The prophet sent his servant to help the boy, but the woman insisted that *Elisha* come to her home: "As the Lord lives, and as you yourself live, I will not leave you" (2 Kings 4:30). As a result of the woman's persistence, Elisha went to her home and with God's power raised the boy from death. Again, persistence resulted in strength and well-being.

Jesus taught us to be persistent in prayer (see Luke 11:1-13). This does not mean nagging or senseless repetition but steadiness, consistency, and frequency in our prayer. The result of such persistence is strength and well-being in our relationship with God and in our particular circumstance and responsibility in this life.

Some Christians set aside an early morning time for scripture reading and prayer, beginning the day in fellowship with the Lord. Others prefer an evening devotional and prayer time, resting and relaxing in the Lord at day's end. Many do both. The secret to strength and confidence in our prayers is daily, steady practice and use of the gift.

Routine does not mean dull. We have a variety of food to nourish our bodies, and we have a wonderful variety of spiritual food, too. Read a whole chapter of Scripture a day, and it will take more than three years to read the whole Bible. Keep a prayer list to notice how many things there are to pray about. Check out the variety of devotionals, commentaries, and prayer books.

Is your prayer life strong? Do you have confidence in your relationship with the Lord, coming to him easily in prayer and speaking to others with ease of his activity in your life? We all need the regular, persistent routine of daily nourishment in Scripture and prayer.

Dear Lord Jesus, you have promised to hear our prayers. You have also promised to give us your Holy Spirit to remind us of your teachings and help us with our prayers. Today we claim all your promises, Lord, and ask you to help us grow daily in our prayer lives. Give us ease and confidence in your presence. Thank you for nourishing us in so many ways.

To learn more about the Shunammite woman and also about prayer:

- Read 2 Kings 4:8-37; 8:1-6.
- Read Ps. 141:1-2; 150; Rom. 8:26-27; Col. 4:2; Phil. 4:4-7; 1 Thess. 5:16-18.
- Establish a regular schedule of Bible reading and prayer. Find a time and place that is convenient and pleasant for you. Then stick with it.

Gratitude That Knows No Bounds
The Widow and Her Penny

And a poor widow came, and put in two copper coins, which make a penny. And [Jesus] called his disciples to him, and said to them, "Truly, I say to you, this poor widow has put in more than all those who are contributing to the treasury. For they all contributed out of their abundance; but she out of her poverty has put in everything she had, her whole living.   Mark 12:42-44

My father-in-law owned a grocery store in Westbrook, Maine. It was a small "mom-and-pop" store, serving the neighborhood. Eddie operated on a very thin profit margin. He had to be competitive in prices in order to attract business away from the supermarkets, but he couldn't buy in huge quantities the way the big stores could. Even so, Eddie would be the first to explain that the Lord had greatly blessed him. Somehow the store had supported his family, even helping to send two youngsters to college, over a period of 35 years.

One of my husband's favorite memories is his father's generosity in giving food away. Westbrook was basically a city built around a paper mill. When a person was employed in the mill, he or she would be assured of a good wage, but layoffs would occur frequently. Then Eddie would see men coming into the store, trying to get up the courage to ask for help in feeding their families. He never turned people away but gave them some sort of help. It sometimes took the form of extended credit; other times it meant just giving away bread and milk. Most of the time Eddie wouldn't be able to collect the large food bills; eventually he would forget them.

One day was particularly bleak for Eddie, because he simply didn't have the money to pay his beef bill. The meat packing company wouldn't send him any more meat until the bill was paid. As he was trying to figure out what to do, Eddie saw a man come into the store who had arranged extended credit on a number of occasions. "Oh, no," Eddie groaned inwardly. "If he needs more help, I'll have to tell him I can't manage it this time." But to Eddie's surprise the man handed him a check. Not only was he paying the money he owed on the groceries, but he had added a little extra, "Just to thank you for helping us when we were down, Mr. Jensen." Eddie's eyes opened wide in amazement: the sum of money in the check was exactly what he needed to pay his beef bill. Once again, the Lord had blessed his giving.

Everything we have is a gift from God. We may think we've earned it and deserve it, but it is only by God's grace that we have food and shelter, necessities and luxuries, money and property, time and talents, family and friends. Scripture teaches that we are stewards of God's gifts. We use them remembering that they really belong to the Lord, and in gratitude we return to him a portion of what he has bestowed on us.

The Jewish temple was a public place. Even the Gentiles were allowed in a large courtyard just outside the temple proper. The Court of the Women was the first area the Jewish men and women would enter; the women would have to stay here, but the men could proceed into the Holy Place. In the Court of the Women were the treasury receptacles, mounted on the wall.

One day Jesus sat in this court watching the people. Rich people were putting large amounts of money into the treasury. And then a poor widow came with her offering. It wasn't much— just two copper coins. But Jesus immediately commended her offering, because in comparison with the others, she had given a tremendous gift—she had given all her money to the Lord. She had literally given up her next meal. And she did it to honor the Lord, trusting him to provide for her. We don't know her name, but we know that she loved and trusted God with all her being.

That is the key to good stewardship—faith and trust in the Lord. In 2 Corinthians Paul describes the attitude of the church in Macedonia in regard to an offering to help the Jerusalem church: "For they gave according to their means, as I can testify, and beyond their means, of their own free will, begging us earnestly for the favor of taking part in the relief of the saints—and this not as we expected, but first they gave themselves to the Lord and to us by the will of God" (8:3-5).

Rather than being "grudge gifts," our offerings to God are to be joyous expressions of love, faith, trust, and gratitude. These gifts of our possessions, time, and talents may not always take the form of offerings to the church but may be gifts to people in need.

We can't outgive God. Eddie was amazed to see the gift returned to him just when he needed the money for his beef. Jesus highly commended the widow's action when she gave all her money to God. Gratitude which knows no bounds is blessed by God's endless grace and love.

Dear Lord and God, forgive our pride and boastfulness when we forget that our every possession is a gift from you. Instead, Lord, fill us with a new realization of your infinite love which shows itself daily. Thank you for the necessary things of life and also for the joyous surprises of unnecessary gifts. Make our attitude one of gratitude instead of selfishness; may we be joyous rather than grudging stewards. Today, Lord, open our hearts and our hands to serve you with our gifts.

To learn more about the poor widow, as well as about stewardship and gratitude:
- Read Mark 12:41-44; 2 Cor. 8:1-15; Luke 12:42-48.
- Treat yourself to a recital of love and joy. Ask Christian friends to share stories about how God has blessed them when they have first given away their time, talents, or possessions. What is your story?

Agree in the Lord
Euodia and Syntyche

I entreat Euodia and I entreat Syntyche to agree in the Lord. And I ask you also, true yokefellow, help these women, for they have labored side by side with me in the gospel together with Clement and the rest of my fellow workers, whose names are in the book of life.   Phil. 4:2-3

Worship at our church in North Hollywood, California, includes drums every Sunday. It also includes an organ, guitars, a choir, pews, folding chairs, green hymnals, a printed worship page, hymns, clapping hands, free-form prayers, introduction of guests, passing the peace, sermons from the pulpit, a sermon given at a music stand, and the sacraments. If this all sounds like a huge jumble, picture this: a congregation made up of people who have been Christian all their lives, as well as people who have recently come to faith in the Lord Jesus; a wide mixture of races, cultures, and ages; a constant inflow of guests and "first timers" to Sunday worship; a decided preference among many people for certain forms of worship.

Presently at our church there are two opportunities for traditional liturgical worship on Sunday morning, as well as one opportunity for a folk service. The music, singing, and forms of worship differ widely between the two services, but the sermon, the prayer concerns, the Scripture, and often the special music are the same.

People express their feelings about the services: "I prefer being in the sanctuary because to me it feels like 'church.' "

"The folk service speaks to me in a way which the more formal service never did."

"Some Sundays I go to the folk service; other Sundays I prefer the formal worship."

The Sunday morning worship at our church is a classic case of "agreeing in the Lord." There are widely differing opinions on what is important in worship, but rather than insisting on only one way of doing things, we have offered options. All the worship services, diverse as they may be, are included within the church, and the pastors are able to move comfortably between them. Soon another option may be offered: Sunday evening services with a combination of traditional and folk worship.

Euodia and Syntyche were two women in the Philippian church who apparently were fighting between themselves. Paul did not state what the fight was about, nor did he take sides. Instead he called on the two women to "agree in the Lord."

One of the beautiful features about people is their individuality. Every person who has ever lived is unique. With this uniqueness and with the gifts of a complex brain and language ability, people have an endless range of ideas and opinions. Environment also comes into play as human beings are shaped and affected in their development. It is unrealistic to expect people to agree on every issue or to think that everyone should agree with *me*. And it is likewise foolish to expect Christians to be uniform in all their opinions. Most church members know that a congregation is often a hotbed of dissension.

But Paul counseled Euodia and Syntyche to "agree in the Lord." Did that mean they must give up their individuality and their uniqueness? Did that mean that they were to become Christian robots? Of course not. To agree in the Lord means that love takes precedence over anger. Sympathy and understanding win out over opinionated stubbornness. Communication, sharing, prayer, and compromise become the way of life. Agreeing in the Lord allows loving, sympathetic discussion to find common ground and agreeable compromises.

At our church people have discovered they can live side by side with both traditional and folk music services. The emphasis is often on the similarities rather than on the differences.

Paul also asked the "true yokefellow," perhaps a pastor of the church, to help the women agree in the Lord. An element of peacemaking and counseling is introduced to encourage fellow

Christians to share their love and sympathy in a difficult situation. This is not to be meddling, but a genuine form of helpful love.

We are human beings; we are believers in the Lord Jesus; we are a forgiven people. But problems and disagreements are bound to arise. Agreeing in the Lord means we are to look for the ways in which we are alike and can agree rather than concentrating on the ways in which we are different. We can celebrate our love and joy in the Lord, extending the hand of peace.

Dear Lord God, we rejoice in our beautiful uniqueness. Thank you for making us special individuals. Lord, our sinful natures propel us into emphasizing our differences with each other rather than our joy and love in you. Help us today to see the ways in which we can "agree in the Lord." Give us the understanding and the patience we need to share your love even in difficult situations. May your Holy Spirit work in and through us as we relate to each other in your kingdom.

To learn more about the Philippian church and about agreeing in the Lord:

- Read Acts 16:11-40. Then read the letter to the Philippians.
- Is there a fellow Christian with whom you are disagreeing? Ask the Lord to give you the words of genuine love and understanding. Then go to that person with agreement and peacemaking on your mind and in your heart.

Compassion Involves Risk
Pharoah's Daughter

Now the daughter of Pharaoh came down to bathe at the river, and her maidens walked beside the river; she saw the basket among the reeds and sent her maid to fetch it. When she opened it she saw the child; and lo, the babe was crying. She took pity on him and said, "This is one of the Hebrews' children."

Exod. 2:5-6

In 1962 my father was invited, along with other clergy, to join Martin Luther King in Albany, Georgia, to protest the treatment of black people. After much prayer my father decided to accept the invitation, despite discouragement from his fellow workers and the news of violence in the South. Many days passed without hearing a word from my father. We anxiously pored over the newspapers and listened to newscasts to learn the fate of the "clergy buses." Finally we heard that my father had been jailed after a peaceful demonstration in front of the courthouse in Albany. The clergy had prayed, sung, and spoken on behalf of black voting rights, and, when they had refused to disperse, they were arrested and jailed.

It was dark in the jail cell where my father was kept with a rabbi, a priest, and another Protestant clergyman. Everything was taken out of his pockets except for his handkerchief, and my father carefully spread that out where his face would touch the dirty cot. He spent several days in jail.

The bail was set at $200, and friends of my father contributed to the fund. It was only in 1980 that the bail money was returned, and so we've said for years that dad was out on bail! It was a symbol of his compassion for others and his deep conviction that black brothers and sisters should be treated fairly. It was an unpopular thing my father did. He was criticized by other pastors and by some people in church leadership positions. But the Rev. Lawrence W. Halvorson protested in the town square and was imprisoned because he hated the injustice he was seeing, and he wanted to do something to help, in Jesus' name.

It sounds contradictory, but it's true that efforts to help other people are not always popular. This is even true in the church, where one would think any effort to help people would be supported and praised. People often risk much to help other human beings.

Pharaoh's daughter came to the Nile River for a bath but left with a son. She spotted the reed basket in which Moses was floating, and when she saw the crying baby "she took pity on him." Her father had issued orders that all male Hebrew babies were to be killed, because the Egyptians were afraid their slaves were becoming too numerous and too powerful. But the Hebrew mothers could not bear to have their children killed and tried to protect them. Moses' mother hid her son for three months and then floated him down the river, probably knowing Pharaoh's daughter would come to bathe. The princess took action on behalf of the baby, even though it meant disobeying and defying her father. Exodus does not tell us about Pharaoh's reaction to all this, but the fact remains that the brave princess had compassion on a baby, compassion which led to an unpopular and even dangerous action.

Compassion can be described as sorrow at the sufferings of another accompanied by a deep urge to help. That sort of response is Christ-like; it is a form of self-denial. It often involves taking risks. Compassion is not a "safe" sort of response. Compassion involves our feelings, our emotions; it involves our time, our energies, our possessions, our family, friends, and acquaintances. It can even involve our reputation and our status in the community.

A child drags a wet, muddy dog into the house. A teenager befriends someone from "the wrong side of the tracks." A family chooses to go to Bangladesh to help people who are sick and starving. A group of people in a church work to establish a Spanish worship service to reach the community. These and other acts of compassion are bound to generate protest. The religious leaders of Jesus' day protested his dealings with the poor, the unclean, and the outcasts of society, too.

Steeped in our concerns, we often look right through people and never really notice them. In Christ we are freed from our own sin and worries in order to be little Christs, actually *seeing* people and their problems and needs. Then we are given grace to reflect and demonstrate God's mercy to them, regardless of the cost. "Walk in love, as Christ loved us and gave himself up for us, a fragrant offering and sacrifice to God" (Eph. 5:2).

Dear Lord Jesus, you gave yourself completely for us helpless, unlovely sinners. Your love and compassion for the world and all its people shone brightly on the cross and in the open tomb. Lord, help us to reflect and share that love and glory with all we meet, seeing people with compassionate eyes. Then, Lord, give us the courage and the energy to help in whatever way we can.

To learn more about Pharaoh's daughter and Moses, as well as about compassion:
- Read Exodus 1 and 2.
- Read Matt. 5:7; 25:31-46; Phil. 2:1-11.
- Today try looking at people. What do you see? What can you do about it? Are you willing to take the risk? Ask the Lord for courage and strength.

Satisfaction Guaranteed
Rachel

Then God remembered Rachel, and God hearkened to her and opened her womb. She conceived and bore a son, and said, "God has taken away my reproach"; and she called his name Joseph, saying "May the Lord add to me another son!"   *Gen. 30:22-24*

A television commercial for carpeting tries to emphasize its five-year guarantee by demonstrating how other things are not guaranteed. A couple stands outside a house for sale asking the realtor if the house is guaranteed. "Guaranteed?" the realtor chortles. "Oh, sure, guaranteed for a lifetime!" Behind him we see the house literally falling apart. The same procedure is followed with a car. "Guaranteed?" the salesman asks with wide eyes. And the automobile caves in while we watch. However, we are solemnly told, satisfaction is guaranteed with the purchase of the carpet. If things go the way they usually do, we will find that we are guaranteed—to be dissatisfied.

We usually are not satisfied with our situation in life. We wish our work, our marriage, our house, our climate, or our government were better.

Dissatisfaction extends into our relationships with other people. We are often unhappy with the way our family members or our friends behave, how they dress, how they talk. I carefully scrutinize the way my boys look when they leave the house, often sending them back to change their shirts or comb their hair. "There," I finally say. "Now I'm satisfied." But I'm usually not. I wish I could make one stand up straight and the other walk correctly.

Furthermore, we are often dissatisfied with ourselves. It may be a physical trait, a personality quirk, or an undependable talent or skill which lets us down. We once had an artist friend who could never finish a painting to his satisfaction. There was always a little detail which needed touching up or correction. Sometimes he would despair over the whole painting and abandon it, starting all over again.

Satisfaction—the state of being content with the way things are —always has to battle our human concept of perfection. On this earth nothing can be perfect, but that's what we want—freedom from any error or flaw.

Rachel, wife of Jacob and sister of Leah, yearned for perfection. As it was, she already had nearly everything a woman in her society might want: beauty, the total love of a man, a secure home. But Rachel was not satisfied. She wanted children, and this caused her to envy her sister and scold her husband. It created deep sorrow and misery for Rachel and led her to offer her maid to Jacob; Bilhah had two sons by him. Legally these babies were Rachel's children, but she wanted to bear her own. Finally Rachel gave birth to a son, but she wanted still more. She even named the boy Joseph which means "he adds," saying "May the Lord add to me another son." Rachel died giving birth to her second son, Benjamin.

Filled as it was with love, security, friends, and even a child, Rachel's life was spent wanting more. In a real sense, her life was wasted. Human beings are like that—never really satisfied. Even as I write this meditation, I'm not satisfied that I'm expressing my real thoughts about it in the best way. I'm now on my third revision.

What is the matter with us? Are we doomed to be dissatisfied with everything and everyone in our lives? Looking at it from the earthly point of view, we can say, "Yes! This dissatisfaction is a direct result of our sinful nature and the imperfect, sinful world in which we live." This is such a discouragement. Most people spend their lives looking for just the right partner, just the right work, just the right living arrangement, just the right— everything.

It's not possible to find satisfaction in earthly relationships, material possessions, or personal worth. There is only one place where true satisfaction is guaranteed—our Lord Jesus Christ. He alone is perfect. He alone will never disappoint us. He alone gives us perfect peace, even amidst all the sorrows and imperfections of this world. And he alone will safely bring us out of this imperfection and into his perfect presence forever.

But what about our time here in this life? Our perfect life with the Lord begins here, and even though our surroundings are imperfect, the Lord will change our attitudes and our reactions toward them. Instead of anger and despair, we can have joy, peace, and patience. Jesus made two promises to his disciples which we, too, can claim: "Peace I leave with you; my peace I give to you; not as the world gives do I give to you. Let not your hearts be troubled, neither let them be afraid (John 14:27). "Lo, I am with you always, to the close of the age" (Matt. 28:20).

Jesus is our Savior, now and forever. He will never fail us. He will give us perfect peace. This is our absolute, certain, unbreakable guarantee!

Dear Lord Jesus, thank you for your rich and bountiful blessings. Too often we don't appreciate any of your gifts but only want more and different ones. Help us train our eyes only on you, Lord Jesus. Help us use our earthly gifts not for our satisfaction but for your glory and for the furtherance of your kingdom.

To learn more about Rachel and also about peace and satisfaction:
- Read Genesis 29; 30:1-24; 35:16-21; Ruth 4:11; Jer. 31:15; Matt. 2:16-18.
- Read Isa. 9:6-7; 48:17-22; Rom. 5:1; Col. 3:15; Ps. 22:3-5.
- Dissatisfaction can become a habit. It's easy to look for the worst. Ask the Lord to reverse the process, helping you look for the best in everything.

Eternal Life because of Christ
Martha of Bethany

Jesus said to her, "I am the resurrection and the life; he who believes in me, though he die, yet shall he live, and whoever lives and believes in me shall never die. Do you believe this?" [Martha] said to him, "Yes, Lord; I believe that you are the Christ, the Son of God, he who is coming into the world."   *John 11:25-27*

My husband's name is well known at various mortuaries in our area. The funeral directors know that Pastor Jensen from that church on Oxnard Avenue will officiate at any funeral at which he is invited to do so. The morticians often express surprise when they learn this about him, because many pastors will officiate only at the funerals of their church members. But my husband learned a long time ago that a funeral is one of his best opportunities for evangelism, for telling the good news about our living Lord and Savior. At the time of a death people are anxious to hear answers to their questions. This is exactly the time a pastor or Christian friend can tell them about Jesus Christ and the possibility of life everlasting through him. The time of death is the best time to talk about life!

Sandy's life was going nowhere. While in her 20s she hadn't thought much about life or death, but when she reached 30, she began noticing how fast the years were going by and how little her life meant. Her child was enrolled in the Christian day school associated with our church, but Sandy had never felt any inclination to be a Christian herself. Then her good friend, Carol, developed lung cancer, and before too many months had passed, the friend died. Sandy was hit especially hard by Carol's death because they were the same age. At Carol's funeral my husband preached the gospel message about life eternal with Jesus Christ, the precious life which begins here and now. Sandy felt as if the pastor were talking directly to her. She'd never heard the gospel presented like that. Suddenly, in the need and openness of the moment, Sandy's heart and mind were filled with the realization of God's love for her. She began worshiping on Sunday mornings and soon asked for Baptism for herself and her child. She was eager to learn more about this Jesus and enrolled in Bible study classes. She served in both the school and church with great joy. She witnessed to her friends about her new faith in the Lord Jesus. Because she had heard about life at the time of death, Sandy's life was completely turned around.

Lazarus had been dead four days when Jesus came to Bethany. His sisters were mourning his death, but Martha hurried to meet Jesus along the road. She had a strong hope and faith: "Lord, if you had been here, my brother would not have died. And even now I know that whatever you ask from God, God will give you" (John 11:21-22). When Jesus told her that he was the resurrection and the life, Martha confessed her faith: "Yes, Lord; I believe that you are the Christ, the Son of God, he who is coming into the world" (John 11:27).

Martha's statement of faith was made before she had any inkling that Jesus would raise her brother from the dead. She believed because Jesus told her who he was, not because of the spectacular miracle. The miracle of Lazarus and his new life became a confirmation of her faith in the here and now.

We do not become Christians because of healing miracles but because of God's Word. Jesus is the visible Word of God. He came to show us what God is like through his life, his death, and his victory over the grave. He showed us God's love and mercy, his incredible grace. Because of Jesus, God will grant us not only eternal life with him in the hereafter, but also a powerful, meaningful existence in this life. Eternal life begins now. We have a hope and faith which enable us to face problems, difficulties, and sorrows as well as joys, successes, and the everyday situations of life on this earth.

Why do we believe such incredible good news? We believe because God has told us it is true and demonstrated it through

Jesus' death and resurrection. This is our eternal hope. "I am the resurrection and the life; he who believes in me, though he die, yet shall he live, and whoever lives and believes in me shall never die." Jesus asks us, just as he asked Martha, "Do you believe this?"

When we believe in Christ, we begin to see the miracles of faith and hope all around us. Our lives take on meaning and delight. Like Martha who hurried to tell Mary about Jesus, we cannot help but share the good news about our Lord with our family, friends, neighbors, and fellow workers. Like Sandy, many of them are waiting to hear the liberating truth: Jesus is alive, and because he lives we, too, shall live eternally. Now there's something worth shouting about!

Dear Lord Jesus, we truly believe that you are the resurrection and the life. Thank you for saving us from our sins and granting us eternal life with you. Make us more aware of our daily walk in life and truth with you, Lord, and give us opportunities to tell others the glorious good news. Together with all believers in every age, we praise and adore you!

To learn more about Martha, Mary, and Lazarus and also about eternal life:
- Read Luke 10:38-42; John 11:1-53; 12:1-11.
- Read John 3:16-21; 12:44-50; 17:1-5; Rom. 5:18-21; 1 John 5:6-13.
- Take time now to think about the message of life eternal in Jesus Christ which you could share with sorrowing friends. Never be insensitive to their grief, but simply share your faith in the Lord Jesus.

Patience in Suffering
Rizpah

The king [David] took the sons of Rizpah the daughter of Aiah, whom she bore to Saul . . . and the five sons of Merab the daughter of Saul, . . . and he gave them into the hands of the Gibeonites, and they hanged them on the mountain before the Lord, and the seven of them perished together. They were put to death in the first days of harvest, at the beginning of barley harvest. Then Rizpah the daughter of Aiah took sackcloth, and spread it for herself on the rock, from the beginning of harvest until rain fell upon them from the heavens; and she did not allow the birds of the air to come upon them by day, or the beasts of the field by night. 2 Sam. 21:8-10

Like many other things in our human lives, grief is a process. It strikes with suddenness but lingers in varying stages of intensity for a long time. The grief process is necessary; shortcuts often lead to physical and emotional problems.

My mother had a seemingly routine operation for gallstones in November 1977, but the surgeon called us into a conference room after the surgery and dropped the bombshell. Instead of gallstones he had found a cancerous, inoperable tumor of the pancreas. I felt as if someone had suddenly socked me in the stomach. I could hardly breathe. The surgeon told us what we could expect and answered a few questions that I, as a nurse, was concerned about. And so the grief process, striking suddenly, began its long journey in my body, mind, and emotions.

After the initial shock my first reaction was denial. They must have made a mistake; this couldn't be cancer! My mother was a "health buff," never smoked or drank alcohol, exercised regularly, ate good food. No, something else was wrong, and soon the doctors would find it. This stage was followed by wretched questioning. Why was this happening to my mother? Why her? Why us? Surprisingly, this questioning passed quickly. I don't think it lasted more than a few hours. And I found myself in anger—"This makes me so mad! It isn't fair!"—and then in resignation to the inevitable. All of these things led into "doing." We thought of many things to help my mother through her personal ordeal, and we made good use of the days left to us.

Four months after the surgery she died. I had already worked through much of my grief, and a new healing, coping, growing stage began. Again, "doing" was important, this time for my own well-being.

The name of Rizpah has become synonymous with suffering. Not only did she have a tragic personal life, but she saw her two sons and five step-grandsons hanged by order of King David. The bodies of the men were left unburied as part of the humiliation and sacrifice. Animals and vultures would be quick to discover the dead bodies and eat them, but Rizpah was determined that this final injustice and indignity would not occur. She kept a vigil by the seven bodies, protecting them and chasing away the predators, even when no one else cared what happened to them. Rizpah kept her lonely, heart-wrenching vigil for five months. It must have been like an endless, dreadful nightmare—the scorching days, the cold frightening nights, the vicious animals, the decomposing bodies.

Finally King David had pity on Rizpah. He realized he must do something not only about the seven bodies but also about the stolen bones of Saul and Jonathan. He recovered the stolen bones and buried them together with the bones of the men who had been hanged. At long last Rizpah's vigil was over, her task accomplished.

There is a passage in Romans which is hard to understand until a person has suffered grief and sorrow: "More than that, we rejoice in our sufferings, knowing that suffering produces endurance, and endurance produces character, and character produces hope, and hope does not disappoint us, because God's love has been poured into our hearts through the Holy Spirit which has been given to us" (Rom. 5:3-5). Here we see a process, a progression. Anyone who has suffered deeply will be quick to say that he or she is a stronger person: character has developed. And the experience of God's faithfulness in a difficult situation assures a person of God's strength and love in the next: hope has been produced.

We do not seek sorrow or suffering, but God can use these human experiences to draw us closer to him, to make us stronger, more effective people. Rizpah was well acquainted with grief and with endurance. Undoubtedly she became a strong woman. I know that my suffering and sorrow have produced a strong person whose faith has grown and who now can relate to other suffering people.

Grieving people need to be loved, to be held closely. They need to be assured of God's love, mercy, and grace. They need to know that grief and mourning are necessary and normal human processes. In time and through patience and dependence on the Lord, God will work the miracles of endurance, character, and hope in suffering people.

Dear Lord God, the pain and sorrow can be so intense that we cry out to you "Why? Why me?" We know that you can do all things; we know that you can use even our sorrows and griefs to your glory. Lord, hold us close. Give us peace and comfort in our painful, difficult days. And then bring light and joy along with character and hope.

To learn more about Rizpah, as well as about sorrow and healing:
- Read 2 Sam. 3:6-11; 21:1-14.
- Read Psalm 13; Psalm 31.
- The book *Good Grief* by Granger Westberg (Fortress Press) is exceptionally helpful for people in sorrow as well as those who are ministering to grieving people.

Being a Peacemaker
Abigail

And David said to Abigail, "Blessed be the Lord, the God of Israel, who sent you this day to meet me! Blessed be your discretion, and blessed be you, who have kept me this day from bloodguilt and from avenging myself with my own hand!"

1 Sam. 25:32-33

The hummingbirds visit our patio frequently, because we have two feeders there for them. What fascinating little birds they are! They appear out of nowhere, their gauzy wings vibrating so fast they're a blur. Sometimes there's a humming sound as they hover; other times the birds move so fast we don't hear a thing. We can always tell when they've been around though, even when we don't see them. The level of red sugar water gets progressively lower, and soon I have to refill the feeders. The hummingbirds are present, doing their work, even when we haven't noticed them.

Peacemakers are often noticed only by the results of their work. Those who smooth the waters, calm the storms, and soothe ruffled feathers are usually unheralded people. They quietly go about their work with loving words, a genuine listening attitude, and wise counsel. Peacemakers do not go out of their way to attract attention to themselves but are often quiet, unassuming people. We notice the results of their peacemaking after they have left.

Being a peacemaker can be very rewarding, but it can also be a difficult and thankless task. In a beautiful way, Jesus commended peacemakers in the beatitudes in the Sermon on the Mount: "Blessed are the peacemakers, for they shall be called sons of God" (Matt. 5:9). Or, as *Today's English Version* states it: "Happy are those who work for peace; God will call them his children!"

Abigail was a beautiful woman. She was married to a difficult, foolish man named Nabal, who was extremely wealthy. He owned 3000 sheep and 1000 goats. Nabal made the mistake of offending David, who was trying to survive with his men as they eluded King Saul. David and his men had helped Nabal's shepherds, protecting them from harm, but when David sent 10 young men to Nabal requesting some food during the feast time, the wealthy man treated them shamefully and sent them away. Nabal's men were horrified; they knew that David's men had helped them.

One of the men went to Abigail, describing the situation. Abigail must have been a wise and organized woman. She immediately sensed the danger in the situation and proceeded to prepare food to bring to David and his men. She loaded the donkeys with 200 loaves of bread, two skins of wine, five dressed sheep, five measures of parched grain, 100 clusters of raisins, and 200 fig cakes. Then, accompanied by a few young men, Abigail traveled toward David.

In the meantime, David's anger was burning, and he vowed to kill Nabal and every man with him. These angry men were on their way to destroy Nabal when Abigail met them. Graciously she apologized to David for her husband's rude and foolish behavior, offering him the food which she had prepared. Abigail also prophesied to David that he would become king and then pointed out that he would not want the blood of Nabal and his men on his conscience when that happened.

Abigail's beautiful, gracious, and brave intercession put out the flame of anger in David. He praised her discretion and her actions, promising not to attack Nabal. Later, after Nabal's death, David remembered this beautiful woman, and Abigail became his wife and the mother of his son Chileab, or Daniel.

Everyone is a peace*lover,* but it takes real grace and strength to be a peace*maker.* Peacemaking involves not only our attitudes but our actions. Peacemakers do not simply spread good will and good cheer but try to create peace where there is hatred and to reconcile separated people. The peacemaker is called upon to modify the positions of people standing at opposite ends of an issue, seeking to dilute the anger, hard feelings, hatred, and distrust.

Jesus Christ was the ultimate peacemaker, reconciling sinful people to God through his life, death, and resurrection. Real peacemaking involves love and selflessness, taking the risk that people may reject you and your efforts. That is the risk Jesus took.

Peacemaking is not interfering, "taking over," or meddling. Peacemaking is bringing God's gracious love into a broken, loveless situation. That is what Christ did for us and what he asks us to do for others.

Dear Lord Jesus, fill us with your love and mercy so we can share it with others. Make us sensitive to people's needs, Lord, and show us what we can do to help. Thank you for bringing perfect peace to this sinful world and for reconciling us with God. May we, like you, be peacemakers in this world.

To learn more about Abigail, as well as about peace:
- Read 1 Samuel 25; 30:1-20; 2 Sam. 3:2-5.
- Read Isa. 26:3-4; 9:6-7; John 14:25-27; Rom. 5:1-11; 14:13-22; 1 Peter 3:8-12.
- Think about specific ways you can be a peacemaker in your circumstances in life. Will it involve smiling, touching, and listening? Will it mean sharing ideas, suggestions, and alternative solutions? Will it include certain actions "above and beyond the call of duty"? Surely it will begin with prayer.

Jesus Christ Turns Us Inside Out
The Samaritan Woman at the Well

The [Samaritan] woman said to him, "I know that Messiah is coming (he who is called Christ); when he comes, he will show us all things." Jesus said to her, "I who speak to you am he." . . . So the woman left her water jar, and went away into the city, and said to the people, "Come, see a man who told me all that I ever did. Can this be the Christ?"   John 4:25-26, 28-29

Krista Marie is now six years old. She's full of life and energy, asks endless questions, and loves music. My brother John thinks Krista is terrific—she's his daughter! John has changed since Krista has been in his life. In many ways John is a softer, mellower, happier person. In a recent letter John wrote:

Krista has given new life to me and to Hjordis. Krista has given me joy, occasional sparkle, and dimensions of childlikeness—most of which wasn't in me before. No, that's not true. It was there, but it was asleep. Or maybe it was afraid to come out into the light of day. Over-seriousness, a strong propensity for cynicism or judgmentalism, a distrust of many social situations, a tendency to think more highly (seriously) of myself than I ought to think—all these rather effectively covered over or anesthetized the parts of me which express a God-given childlikeness. Krista's presence in my life, her love for me, have awakened some of these dormant realities. She has helped me discover not only flowers, rocks, snails, and animals (they were there before, I just didn't see them), but also trust, carefreeness, and a lighter, more festive, more happy side of life.

As human beings we are naturally turned in on ourselves. It's part of our sinful, broken nature. It shows itself in selfishness, preoccupation with our own problems, concentration on what's good for us, hurting others in order to achieve our own goals. In the process of such selfish living we suffer the results of our sin and brokenness. And the painful results continue to turn us in on ourselves, concentrating all the more on our problems and our selfish plans. We become hopelessly tied up in our sin, totally unable to save ourselves. What's more, we do not naturally possess any interest or inclination to turn to God to save us. We are in complete rebellion against God.

The Samaritan woman came to the well at noon time. Her sin and brokenness kept her away from the well in the evening when the other women of the village would come to draw water. She preferred to come when no one else was there. But someone was at the well that day—a Jewish man. "Give me a drink," Jesus asked the woman. And that was the beginning of a long conversation which led the Samaritan woman to confess her sin and begin to focus on Jesus as the Messiah.

Hope welled up in the woman, and even before she was completely sure of what she was hearing and seeing, she rushed into the village to tell the people about Jesus. "Come, see a man who told me all that I ever did. Can this be the Christ?" She turned the Samaritans' attention to Jesus "and many more believed because of his word. . . . They said to the woman, 'It is no longer because of your words that we believe, for we have heard for ourselves, and we know that this is indeed the Savior of the world'" (John 4:41-42).

The Samaritan woman had come to the well in the hot, noonday sun in order to avoid the other women, but after talking to Jesus she could not keep the good news to herself. The Messiah had begun to turn the woman inside out.

Inside out! That's what Jesus does to our lives. His Holy Spirit works the miracles of repentance and healing. The tenseness, rigidity, and selfishness give way to peace, joy, and interest in other people. Through his love in dying for our sin and rising to conquer death and the devil, Jesus Christ has freed us from the hopeless, deadly treadmill in which we have been trapped. As freed people we joyfully worship Christ and willingly serve others.

Krista has shown John what it means to live in joy and happiness. She brings my brother not only delight in his daughter but a new outlook on all of life. Seeking only a jarful of water at noon time, the Samaritan woman received the living water which not only cleansed her but spilled over in a joyful flood to the people in the village. Jesus Christ gives us the true joy and the true peace we crave. He turns us inside out, away from ourselves and toward God, worshiping our Lord and Savior and serving our fellow human beings.

Dear Jesus Christ, you are the Living Water, the one who cleanses us from all our sins. Thank you for turning our lives inside out, for freeing us from the trap of sin and death. And now, Lord, make us aware of the needs of other people. We want to serve you by serving others. Keep our eyes and hearts focused clearly on you and on your love for us.

To learn more about the Samaritan woman and about our salvation:

- Read John 4:1-42; Luke 10:25-37; Acts 8:4-8. Samaritans and Jews hated each other. Note how Christ turned the situations around.
- First read Rom. 7:7-25. Then read Rom. 8:1-39. Praise God for your salvation in Jesus Christ.
- Now turn to serve another person in Jesus' name. Thank the Lord for being "inside out."

Costly Love
Mary of Bethany

Mary took a pound of costly ointment of pure nard and anointed the feet of Jesus and wiped his feet with her hair; and the house was filled with the fragrance of the ointment.   John 12:3

But Jesus said, "Let her alone; why do you trouble her? She has done a beautiful thing to me. . . . She has done what she could; she has anointed my body beforehand for burying. And truly, I say to you, wherever the gospel is preached in the world, what she has done will be told in memory of her."   Mark 14:6, 8-9

Eddie gave up his life for Carrie. It happened so gradually that we didn't realize it until after his death.

We lived in Minnesota, and my parents-in-law, Eddie and Carrie, lived in Maine. Carrie had been fighting skin and bone cancer for several years until a leg had to be amputated. Eddie took care of his wife, fixing up the little apartment so she could use the kitchen and manage the narrow hallway to the bedroom and bathroom. Carrie required a lot of help with her prosthesis, the wheelchair, and the crutches. Countless visits were made to the hospital, doctor, and drugstore.

By 1978 Carrie was receiving chemotherapy. "Everything's fine," Eddie assured us in the capable voice we knew so well. "In fact, we're coming to see you and Dot and all the grandchildren." And so they did. Eddie seemed to be fighting a bad cold while visiting Dot and Jim in Nebraska, but he refused to go to the doctor. He insisted on getting to Minneapolis with Carrie.

Everyone was so happy when Carrie and Eddie finally arrived! We all had the sense that this would be Carrie's last visit to our home, and we wanted to make every moment count. Three hours after their arrival Eddie suffered a stroke; 16 hours later he died of a massive heart attack. The autopsy showed that he had previously experienced many small heart attacks and that the vessels of the heart muscle were nearly closed. Eddie apparently refused to seek care for himself because Carrie needed him. His love for her was very costly.

It's easy to criticize people for giving so completely of themselves. We've often wondered why Eddie didn't go to the doctor. Was he afraid he'd be hospitalized and there'd be no one to care for his wife? We don't know the answer. But we can say of Eddie, as we can say of dedicated missionaries and of heroes in disasters, that he was willing to make the costly sacrifice.

Mary of Bethany was criticized, too. She used a whole flask of costly ointment to anoint Jesus. People gathered in Simon's house said, "Why was the ointment thus wasted? For this ointment might have been sold for more than three hundred denarii, and given to the poor" (Mark 14:4-5). It really did seem like such a foolish thing to do. But Jesus commended Mary for her love which did not count the cost to herself. "She has done what she could; she has anointed my body beforehand for burying." Then he said that Mary of Bethany would be remembered in the gospel story for her act of costly love. And we do remember her.

True love does not count the cost to itself but gives itself completely on behalf of others. The most perfect example of such love is Jesus Christ. In Philippians 2:5-8 Paul tells about Jesus' loving sacrifice:

Have this mind among yourselves, which you have in Christ Jesus, who, though he was in the form of God, did not count equality with God a thing to be grasped, but emptied himself, taking the form of a servant, being born in the likeness of men. And being found in human form he humbled himself and became obedient unto death, even death on a cross.

We are called to love Christ as he loves us—completely and unreservedly. And then we are called to share such unreserved love with other people. We are often afraid to do this, because it is very risky. What if people scorn us or laugh at us? What if they ignore us or, worse yet, take advantage of us? What if it costs more than we had planned to give?

Complete and unreserved love does not ask these questions. Rather, it gives as Christ has given to us—totally, with nothing held back. "This is my commandment, that you love one another as I have loved you. Greater love has no man than this, that a man lay down his life for his friends" (John 15:12-13). "He who loses his life for my sake will find it" (Matt. 10:39).

Dear Lord Jesus, you have loved us with complete, unreserved love, but we cannot comprehend such true love. Thank you for pouring it out upon us even when we do not understand. Lord, take away our fear of giving costly love to others. Help us concentrate only on your perfect love and grace, remembering your sacrifice for us.

To learn more about Mary of Bethany and about costly love:
- Read John 11:1—12:11; Matt. 26:6-13; Mark 14:3-9.
- Costly love is totally unselfish love for another. Talk with a Christian friend about it. What are some ways it can be practiced? Pray together about them.

Jesus Christ Is Lord
Jezebel

And Ahab the son of Omri did evil in the sight of the Lord more than all that were before him. And as if it had been a light thing for him to walk in the sins of Jeroboam the son of Nebat, he took for wife Jezebel the daughter of Ethbaal king of the Sidonians, and went and served Baal, and worshiped him.

1 Kings 16:30-31

During a recent journey in Egypt I wandered through many temples and tombs where the carvings and hieroglyphs are still very clear even after three and four thousand years. Many of the carvings and statues are of the ancient Egyptian gods such as Horus, Hathor, Isis, and Osiris, as well as the pharaohs who were worshiped as gods. Weather and time have worn down some of the carvings, leaving them smooth and ill-defined, but I was startled to see actual vandalism on some of the faces on the statues. The guides explained that early Christians had defaced and destroyed many of the carvings in an attempt to stamp out idol worship. Part of me understood the effort, sharing the abhorrence of a false god, but part of me was saddened to see the destruction of ancient art.

The truth about idol worship, of course, is that it cannot be stamped out by defacing a statue. That's because false gods are all about us and within us, even today. A false god is anything which occupies center stage in our lives beside the true God. In our day that can include success, money, property, fame, and power, as well as things which seem good in themselves, such as family, work, physical well-being, and recreation.

We also need to recognize that the "old" false gods are still with us. A 1980 feature article in a Los Angeles newspaper described the practice of witchcraft. A "witch" stated that the

Mother Goddess, the giver of life, has been known by many names over the centuries including Isis, Astarte, Ashtaroth, and Mother Nature. In ancient Israel both Baal and Ashtaroth were worshiped as fertility god and goddess. Incredible as it seems, this kind of worship is still going on today.

King Ahab married a princess, but the story which followed was anything but an idlyllic fairy tale. Jezebel was a worshiper of Baal and brought her religion with her into the palace of Israel in the ninth century B.C. Ahab also became a worshiper of Baal, and the stage was set for idolatry, cruelty, injustice, stealing, and murder. Ahab ruled over Israel for 22 years, and Jezebel was whispering in his ear all that time.

Elijah the prophet was the voice of God's judgment to Ahab and Jezebel. Elijah preached about the sin of Baal worship and predicted the ugly deaths of both the king and queen if they did not repent. Eventually Ahab was killed in battle, and the dogs licked up his blood, just as Elijah had said. Jezebel continued her evil influence in Israel through her children for 14 more years but finally met a gruesome death, fulfilling Elijah's prophecy that the dogs would eat her.

The name of Jezebel has become a symbol of wickedness and idolatry. Revelation 2:20 names a woman in Thyatira as "Jezebel" because she was leading people into immorality and idolatry. At one time any woman who "painted her face" was called a Jezebel, a reference to 2 Kings 9:30 where Jezebel "painted her eyes, and adorned her head" in preparation for Jehu's visit just before her death. But Jezebel's sin was not the way she made up her face. It was her worship of a false god and her influencing other people to follow.

Think of a large wagon wheel. Visualize the hub in the center from which the spokes go out to meet the rim. If our lives can be compared to that wheel, the Lord asks to be the hub. He asks that all worship be concentrated on him and that everything in our lives touch him and fan out from him. The spokes of the wheel can be regarded as important aspects of our lives: family, work, finances, leisure, hobbies, and many more. We have a false god if anything beside the Lord Jesus Christ is at the hub of our lives, if anything or anyone else has more influence on us than Christ.

The good news is that Jesus Christ has won the victory over every false god, over sin, death, and the power of the devil. Yes, we still live in the physical world where we are drawn and tugged from many sides by many influences, but God's Holy Spirit has promised to live with us in the struggle. He will enable us to identify the false gods we hold dear and to put them away from any position of worship. Jesus Christ is to be first, foremost, and central. As we surrender our false gods and by God's grace let Jesus be the hub of our lives, we will discover the joy and the peace that come from his loving and saving presence. When Jesus Christ is Lord, all aspects of our lives will fall naturally into place. Our words and actions will proclaim Christ's lordship to others.

Dear Lord Jesus, we live in a constant struggle between the power of evil and the power of your love and mercy. May your Holy Spirit dwell in us, giving us strength and grace to remain strong in faith and love toward you. Help us always to worship you in truth. Keep us from false gods and prophets. May our lives be beautiful and sweet in your love, and may our influence on others always direct their thoughts and lives toward the one God, our Lord Jesus Christ.

To learn more about Jezebel, as well as about Jesus, the center of our lives:

- Read 1 Kings 16:29-33; 18; 19:1-3; 21–22. Also 2 Kings 9 and 10.
- Read Matt. 6:24-34; Rom. 8:9-17, 26-28.
- Draw a wagon wheel. Write "Jesus Christ" on the hub. Name the spokes with the important aspects of your life. Note how all these aspects come from Christ and how they all touch Christ. What meaning does this have for our prayer lives?

Let Me Tell You about Jesus!
Priscilla

After this Paul stayed many days longer, and then took leave of the brethren and sailed for Syria, and with him Priscilla and Aquila. . . . And they came to Ephesus and he left them there. . . . [Apollos] began to speak boldly in the synagogue; but when Priscilla and Aquila heard him, they took him and expounded to him the way of God more accurately. Acts 18:18-19, 26

BEGINNING BIBLE CLASS WILL START NEXT WEEK.
BEGINNING BIBLE STUDENTS WILL USE THE GOOD NEWS BIBLE.
BEGINNING BIBLE MEETS UPSTAIRS, THIRD DOOR TO THE RIGHT.

Certainly it wasn't an original discovery, but it was a new idea to us. It took an evangelism conference to make us realize that many people joining our church, as well as many people already in the church, needed to have a simple, start-right-at-the-beginning type of Bible class. Simple as the idea was, it struck us right from the blue. We had been guilty of assuming that everyone coming to church had a Sunday school and confirmation level of Bible understanding. Not true, not true!

Betty taught the first Beginning Bible class, and she described it as a wonderful delight: "What fun to watch the lights go on in their eyes as they suddenly see the Word of God come to life!" Betty was having a "Priscilla" experience.

Chased out of Rome because they were Jews, Priscilla and Aquila had come to Corinth to practice their trade of tentmaking. They hadn't been there long when Paul, also a tentmaker, came to Corinth. From the apostle the couple heard the gospel message about Jesus. This wasn't a mere Sunday activity for Priscilla and Aquila, but a life-changing experience. They became evangelists, tellers of the good news.

When Paul sailed for Syria, he took Priscilla and Aquila with

114

him, dropping them off in Ephesus to begin evangelism work. It must have been a frightening and overwhelming task. Ephesus was a pagan city with much idolatry and immorality. But Priscilla and her husband went to work. Empowered by the Holy Spirit, they established a "house church" and began building the foundations for a strong mission.

One day Apollos came to Ephesus, teaching about Jesus. Priscilla and Aquila were alarmed to hear only a partial message from him; he apparently did not know about Jesus' death and resurrection. So the two evangelists took Apollos aside and carefully taught him the beautiful, complete message about Jesus and his saving life, death, and resurrection. Apollos went on to become a powerful preacher of the gospel.

What a joy it is to tell the good news about Jesus! But we often are afraid to do so, especially to people outside our families and our churches. They might think we're weird or fanatic, we tell ourselves. What we don't realize is that many people are waiting to hear the good news of life eternal in Jesus Christ.

My father, a pastor, was traveling on a bus from New York to Philadelphia. In visiting with his seatmate, my father discovered he was Jewish. Not wanting to offend the older man but feeling compelled to speak, my father reached into his pocket and took out a copy of the gospel of Matthew. "I'd like to give this to you," he said, handing the book to the Jewish man. "It's the good news about Jesus Christ and the salvation available to you in him." Expecting a heated refusal, my father was amazed to see tears trickling from the man's eyes as he accepted the little book. "I have waited so very long for someone to tell me about Jesus," the man said. "I have many Christian friends and neighbors, but no one has ever talked to me about Jesus before."

No one likes pushy, aggressive, unpleasant people to tell them anything, certainly not the message of salvation. But a person who lives in the power of Christ's Spirit and prays for open doors to talk about his or her faith will discover that the Lord has prepared the way. Priscilla probably wished she were anywhere but in the pagan city of Ephesus; my dad could hardly believe that such a special opportunity came on a bus; Betty was nervous about teaching Beginning Bible. But the Lord blesses evangelism efforts done in his name and for his sake. He pours out his Spirit in abundance.

Ask today for the words and the opportunities to speak about Jesus. It may be a message of hope to unbelievers; it may be words of faith and encouragement to new believers; it may be a matter of telling the "old, old story" to people who have known and loved it but who need to hear it again. We are Christ's body on this earth, and that means we are his voice, his smile, and his touch for everyone we meet.

Dear Lord Jesus, you know that we often become speechless in situations which need your beautiful message of salvation. Loosen our tongues and give us the courage and power of your Holy Spirit. Lord, open hearts and minds to your life-giving message, and may we be the messengers of your love and salvation.

To learn more about Priscilla and Aquila, as well as about telling the good news:
- Read Acts 18:1-21, 24-28; Rom. 16:3-5.
- Read Acts 2:1-37; 4:1-31; 8:4-8; 10:34-48.
- God equips us for service. Read Eph. 6:10-20. Make a sketch of the soldier, marking the equipment with the names of God's gifts. When he asks us to serve, the Lord gives strength and protection.

Trusting in God's Promises
Deborah

[Deborah] sent and summoned Barak . . . and said to him, "The Lord, the God of Israel, commands you, 'Go, gather your men at Mount Tabor, taking ten thousand from the tribe of Naphtali and the tribe of Zebulun. And I will draw out Sisera, the general of Jabin's army, to meet you by the river Kishon with his chariots and his troops; and I will give him into your hand.'" . . . And Barak summoned Zebulun and Naphtali to Kedesh; and ten thousand men went up at his heels; and Deborah went up with him.   Judg. 4:6-7, 10

First-day activities after major abdominal surgery included dangling my feet while sitting on the edge of the hospital bed and then, with lots of help from the nurse, walking a short distance to the chair. I visited with the nurse and nurse's aide as they made my bed.

Then suddenly the dangling, the walking, and the conversation caught up with me, and I felt very dizzy. Everything began to go black in front of my eyes, and a roaring sound began to fill my ears. "I'm going to faint," I announced to my audience and leaned toward the floor. "I'm going . . . I'm going . . ."

The two women grabbed me and told me firmly that I was *not* going to faint. "Come on," they said, "you're going back to bed. Look up! Keep looking up! Don't look down!" as they propelled me to the bed. I was obedient and kept looking up. The words of encouragement, the good advice, and the firm grip saved the day. I indeed did not faint. What's more, later in the day I was walking by myself.

Deborah would not let Barak look down either. First she explained to the Israelite general what the Lord was asking of him, namely, to gather troops to fight the Canaanite army commanded by Sisera. This must have been fearsome news for Barak, because the Canaanites were very strong. They not only had many troops, but they also had 900 chariots of iron. King Jabin had oppressed the people of Israel for 20 years, and now the Lord was asking Barak to do battle with the powerful Sisera and his army.

But Deborah wasn't finished. There was a promise to go along with the command: the Lord pledged to give the Israelites the victory, delivering Sisera into Barak's hand.

Deborah was a judge in ancient Israel. She acted as both an arbiter of problems and as a prophet of the Lord. Deborah would sit under a palm tree (which came to be known as the palm of Deborah), and there would make her judgments. She was a brave woman. When Barak would not go into battle without her by his side, Deborah didn't flinch, but trusted God's promise. Deborah accompanied Barak to Mount Tabor, where the Israelite troops were gathered, and became a symbol of God's promise and God's presence in the fearsome battle.

And as Deborah believed it would happen, the Lord gave a great victory to Barak and the Israelites. Despite the tremendous odds against them, the Israelites defeated the Canaanites and were free once again. The people praised God for keeping his promise.

How easy it is to become discouraged in our daily lives as seemingly insurmountable problems surround us! Often the problems multiply faster than we can begin to solve them. The yoke is heavy about our necks, forcing us to look down, down. All we see is gloom, sorrow, and destruction. Like Peter walking on the water, we look down and see the dangerous murky depths. Like Peter, we feel ourselves sinking.

At this point God speaks his wonderful promises of hope and faith. Nothing is too big or too terrible for our Lord. He asks us to trust him, to look upward to him and his promises. Like Peter, when we keep our eyes on the Lord we experience God's marvels —we "walk on the water"!

Listen to some of the beautiful promises of the Lord:

"Lo, I am with you always, to the close of the age" (Matt. 28:20).

"But the Lord is faithful; he will strengthen you and guard you from evil" (2 Thess. 3:3).

"We know that in everything God works for good with those who love him, who are called according to his purpose" (Rom. 8:28).

"What then shall we say to this? If God is for us, who is against us? . . . For I am sure that neither death, nor life, nor angels, nor principalities, nor things present, nor things to come, nor powers, nor height, nor depth, nor anything else in all creation, will be able to separate us from the love of God in Christ Jesus our Lord" (Rom. 8:31, 38-39).

Look up! Don't look down! Keep your eyes firmly and trustingly on the Lord and his promises! You will be blessed not only with the fulfillment of the promises but with the strength and peace of God holding you up in your daily walk through life.

Dear heavenly Father, help us keep our eyes and our hearts fixed on you and your promises. Thank you for the possibility of victorious living now and in all eternity because of Jesus. Give us your grace to claim the promises of your presence and your strength in our daily lives. Let us be channels of your love and grace to everyone we meet. Thank you for loving us and being faithful to your promises.

To learn more about Deborah and Peter and to hear more of God's promises:
- Read Judges 4 and 5.
- Read Matt. 14:22-23.
- Read 2 Peter 3:8-9; Matt. 7:7-8; Heb. 13:8, 14; Matt. 11:28-30; Isa. 42:16; Psalm 139; Matt. 6:25-34.
- Write down a promise of the Lord which is especially meaningful to you. Place it where you will often see it. Memorize it. Share it with someone.

What Is Truth?
Sapphira

But a man named Ananias with his wife Sapphira sold a piece of property, and with his wife's knowledge he kept back some of the proceeds, and brought only a part and laid it at the apostles' feet.   Acts 5:1-2

Illusions of truth are all about us. Living in North Hollywood, I have come to know many people in the film and television industry and have had a chance to see how films are made. I have great admiration for the skills of the film editors and those who make and film miniatures and scale models. They create an illusion of truth on the screen by cutting, splicing, and careful craftsmanship. Such illusions are meant for our enjoyment.

Other illusions of truth can be very damaging. Just a few days ago I found a card with the following message on my car's windshield:

Sister Sonya, Natural Born Spiritual Psychic Reader and Advisor: There is no problem so great that she can't solve. Tells you how to hold your job, when you have failed and how to succeed. Calls your friends and enemies by name without asking a single word. Will tell you your troubles and what to do about them. Reunites the separated. Guaranteed to remove evil influences and bad luck. . . . Lifts you out of sorrow and darkness and starts you on the way to success and happiness. She is here for the first time in this vicinity; has just come from Egypt, the land of miracles. What your eyes will see, your heart will believe. . . . Half price with this ad.

And in the left-hand corner of the card was a picture of Jesus.
All of us are good at creating our own illusions of the truth.

Even when we might not actually intend to lie, we talk around a subject or tell what we call "white lies" or "half-truths." And when we lie, it's usually to protect our self-interests. Even when we rationalize by saying we're doing it for someone else, the bottom line says, "This is best for me and mine."

The people in the first community of believers in Jerusalem had all things in common. Many people sold their possessions and goods, then brought the proceeds to the apostles, who helped distribute them to those in need. Ananias and Sapphira sold a piece of property but decided to keep some of the money for themselves. They also decided to keep this a secret, declaring to the apostles that they had sold the property for the amount which was given to the church. Peter detected the lie immediately and challenged Ananias: "Why has Satan filled your heart to lie to the Holy Spirit? . . . How is it that you have contrived this deed in your heart? You have not lied to men but to God" (Acts 5:3-4).

The results of the lie were immediate and startling. When Peter spoke to him about the lie, Ananias fell down dead. When Sapphira came in about three hours later, Peter questioned her closely. Sapphira told the same lie her husband had told. And then she, too, dropped dead. The young men who had buried Ananias now carried out Sapphira to be buried beside him. It's no wonder that "great fear came upon the whole church, and upon all who heard of these things" (Acts 5:11).

The people in the early church needed to know that the God of all truth expected truthfulness from them, not lying and deception. They were the first fruits of Pentecost, Christ's body here on earth. Sapphira and her husband became examples of how important the message of truth really was.

What is truth? In our sinful world nothing is perfectly truthful. Only God, who is holy and perfect in every way, can be said to be "the Truth." Jesus Christ, the Son of God, declared himself to be "the way, and the truth, and the life" (John 14:6). Jesus is the way to the perfect truth and eternal life which is God. Through him we can know and experience the truth of our existence. The truth is that God created us and that he loved us so much, even

121

in our sinfulness, that he sent his Son Jesus to live among us, to die and to be raised again—all so that we can live with God forever in grace and in truth.

Such truth is staggering! It frees us from fears and selfishness, allowing us to be what God intends us to be—his loving people living in community with others. In such a life of caring there is no room for deceit and dishonesty. Truth is the norm and is to be shared in mercy and love. This peaceful, joyous, trusting attitude comes only from God—and he is the truth on which we can depend for all eternity.

Dear God of all truth, your Son Jesus Christ is the way, the truth, and the life. Thank you for saving us for all eternity through his life-giving death and resurrection. Lord, keep us from lying and deceit, and help us live in merciful and loving truth.

To learn more about Ananias, Sapphira, and the early church, as well as about truth:

- Read Acts 2:41-47; 4:32—5:11.
- Read John 8:31-32; 14:1-11. Note how Jesus directs everyone to God.
- Examine your vocabulary. Do terms like "white lies," "half-truths," and "let's-not-tell-the-whole-story" ever crop up? Ask the Lord to help you speak the truth in love. By word and example teach children in your care to do the same.

The Word of God Has Power
Lydia

*And on the sabbath day we went outside the gate to the river-
side, where we supposed there was a place of prayer; and we sat
down and spoke to the women who had come together. One who
heard us was a woman named Lydia, from the city of Thyatira, a
seller of purple goods, who was a worshiper of God. The Lord
opened her heart to give heed to what was said by Paul. And
when she was baptized, with her household, she besought us,
saying, "If you have judged me to be faithful to the Lord, come to
my house and stay." And she prevailed upon us.   Acts 16:13-15*

One of the most important things I have learned is that the
Word of God has power, in and of itself. I used to worry about
whether I had presented Bible studies in such a way that the
Word would have effect. Somehow the pressure was on *me* to
make sure the Word was powerful. What a relief, what a tremendous *freedom* I felt when a seminary professor assured me
that my task was to sow the seed and preach the good news, not
agonize over whether it had "worked." Now I knew how my
father, my brother, and my husband could preach every Sunday
without becoming emotional and spiritual basket cases!

I've seen this truth in action as I've taught in our church's lay
school of theology. This branch of our adult Christian education
program offers classes in Bible, church history, and practical
Christianity. I have the joyful freedom to present the electrifying
gospel message, knowing that God will work the miracle. I have
observed the fruits of the Spirit manifest themselves and watched
Christian service develop in students who are deep in the Word.
It's a great joy—but no surprise—to see that new church school
teachers and aides are coming out of the lay school, as well as new
members of key church committees. I'm delighted—but not sur-

prised—to see the lay school students faithfully worshiping and bringing family and friends to church with them. The Word of God is working mightily and powerfully!

Lydia was a businesswoman in Philippi. On the sabbath day she would go to the place of prayer by the riverside to worship God. It was here that Lydia heard the good news from Paul about Jesus and his life, death, and resurrection. The apostle was undoubtedly a dynamic speaker, but it was the *words* he was saying that were important. "The Lord opened her heart to give heed to what was *said* by Paul." It's obvious that the Word of God had a strong and immediate effect on Lydia because two things happened: she was baptized in the name of Jesus in the nearby river, and she began serving the Lord by ministering to Paul and the company of people with him. This seller of purple goods quickly manifested the fruits of the Spirit and discipleship.

Such examples of the power of God's Word are found all through Scripture, and through the history of the church. The examples are all about us, if we only notice them.

When we know that the Word of God has power, we can see that our task is to make the Word known to as many people as possible. Organizations like the American Bible Society suddenly take on new value. Now we can understand why it's important to publish and distribute the Word of God. Bringing people to Bible studies and to worship services becomes of paramount importance when we understand that it's not only the written Word but the spoken and interpreted Word of God that has power. Ministering to others is a crucial activity, not only because it helps people but because the Word of God has power in the ministry of believers, too.

The Apostle Paul knew that he was not responsible for the miracles of faith and growth. To the people at Corinth Paul wrote, "What then is Apollos? What is Paul? Servants through whom you believed, as the Lord assigned to each. I planted, Apollos watered, but God gave the growth" (1 Cor. 3:5-6). The knowledge that God worked the miracle of faith through his Word was undoubtedly Paul's impetus to keep working, keep traveling, keep preaching. Lydia and many other people came to faith because of God's Word brought to them by Paul.

How can *you* spread God's Word? Will it mean reading the Scripture with your family? teaching in church schools? reading the Scripture lessons in the worship service? giving away New Testaments or Scripture portions? sharing favorite Bible verses with fellow workers and friends? Remember—all you are asked to do is plant the seed of God's Word. The Lord will work the miracle of faith through his holy and precious Word.

Dear Lord, what beautiful promises you have made through your Word! What a priceless salvation you have given to us in your grace! Give us opportunities to share Jesus Christ, your Word to this world, with family, friends, neighbors, co-workers, and even strangers. Help us sow the seed, Lord. We pray for your miraculous gift of growth.

To learn more about Lydia and about the Word of God:
- Read Acts 16:6-40. Then read the letter to the Philippians with great joy!
- Read Ps. 119:89-112; Isa. 40:8; Deut. 8:3 and Matt. 4:1-4; John 1:1, 14; 2 Tim. 3:14—4:5.
- How can *you* spread God's Word in your particular situation? Be specific!

Humility and Honor
Phoebe

I commend to you our sister Phoebe, a deaconess of the church at Cenchreae, that you may receive her in the Lord as befits the saints, and help her in whatever she may require from you, for she has been a helper of many and of myself as well.   Rom. 16:1-2

"Well done, good and faithful servant; . . . enter into the joy of your master" (Matt. 25:21). These words from one of Jesus' parables have taken on special meaning for me since Ralph Hanke's funeral.

Whenever I think of Ralph, I see him serving other people. This man of God with the beautiful smile and dancing eyes was always doing something for someone else. One of the last times I saw Ralph he was sweeping the parish hall floor after a huge talent show which had raised funds for World Hunger projects. He thoroughly enjoyed the program, and even though there were younger people around to sweep, Ralph wanted to serve, too. I can see him in the parsonage patio, digging in the rock-hard soil, trying to cultivate it so I could have flowers outside my living room window. He did it, too, planting ferns, azaleas, camellias, gardenias, and fuchsia. Ralph served on the call committee when my husband became senior pastor at our church. His encouraging words made us feel so welcome. And as a member of the evangelism committee Ralph called on families in the community. He once told me his greatest joy was to share with other people what Jesus Christ meant to him, inviting them to faith, too. Ralph was a servant in a day when servanthood isn't very popular. And now he's with the Lord, having entered into the joy of his master.

Phoebe was a believer in Christ who lived in the Greek port city of Cenchreae. Paul refers to her as a "deaconess" of that church. Deaconess has been translated as "servant." Phoebe apparently served the church in some special capacity, perhaps ministering to the sick. Phoebe was traveling, and Paul sent his wonderful commendation with her. He asked the church she visited to "receive her in the Lord as befits the saints." Paul said Phoebe had been a helper of many, including himself. Phoebe was a faithful servant of God, ministering to other people in a day when such servanthood was not common. Because of her servanthood she was commended and honored by Paul.

Everyone likes honor and recognition, but hardly anyone likes the role of a servant. Somehow that sounds demeaning. But our Lord Jesus taught that he had come to serve and that those who follow him are also to be servants: "Whoever would be first among you must be your slave; even as the Son of man came not to be served but to serve, and to give his life as a ransom for many" (Matt. 20:27-28).

In his life Jesus demonstrated his servanthood. He fed people. He healed their illnesses and listened to their problems. He rejoiced with them. He sorrowed with them. Jesus served people when he himself was weary. In the temple he showed that his servanthood was not passive but could become fierce when faced with injustice (Mark 11:15-19). Finally Jesus' servanthood took the form of suffering and death on the cross for the sake of redeeming all sinners. His life was given as a ransom for many.

When Jesus sent his disciples out to preach the good news of the kingdom of heaven, he taught that a disciple is to be like his teacher. And so Jesus told his disciples that each one should take up his cross and follow him; the disciples who did this would be worthy of their teacher. Jesus said, "He who finds his life will lose it, and he who loses his life for my sake will find it" (Matt. 10:39).

These are difficult words for us. To understand them we need to think in terms of our own lives and our own circumstances. What would Christ have us do there? What service could be performed in Jesus' name? What talents do we have which would help in a certain situation? It is in noticing the day-by-day needs of those in our family, our neighborhood, our church, and our community that we see specifically what our servant role is to be.

And it is in being faithful, obedient servants of Christ that we will be commended by our Savior. Honor does not come to those who seek it but rather to those who serve. "Well done, good and faithful servant; . . . enter into the joy of your master!"

Lord Jesus, we want to live in your presence for all eternity. We want to serve you but it seems so hard to be a servant in our daily lives. Lord, show us day by day what you want us to do. Open the opportunities of service, giving us the desire and ability to help other people, right where we are. We want to be good and faithful servants.

To learn more about Jesus' servanthood and our role as servants:
- Read Isaiah 53. Describe the Messiah's servanthood.
- Read 1 Peter 2:18-25. All of us are servants. What do you learn about servanthood? Now read 1 Peter 5:10-11.
- With a Christian friend discuss servanthood in Christ. What implications does it have in both your lives? Pray for each other and continue to encourage each other as you serve the Lord.